How To Write In Plain English

A Writing Guide That Saves Time, Is Easy to Read and Helps Readers Understand Your Message

Nicole Foster

© **Copyright 2022 - All rights reserved.**

The content contained within this book may not be reproduced, duplicated or transmitted without direct written permission from the author or the publisher.

Under no circumstances will any blame or legal responsibility be held against the publisher, or author, for any damages, reparation, or monetary loss due to the information contained within this book, either directly or indirectly.

Legal Notice:

This book is copyright protected. It is only for personal use. You cannot amend, distribute, sell, use, quote or paraphrase any part, or the content within this book, without the consent of the author or publisher.

Disclaimer Notice:

Please note the information contained within this document is for educational and entertainment purposes only. All effort has been executed to present accurate, up to date, reliable, complete information. No warranties of any kind are declared or implied. Readers acknowledge that the author is not engaged in the rendering of legal, financial, medical or professional advice. The content within this book has been derived from various sources. Please consult a licensed professional before attempting any techniques outlined in this book.

By reading this document, the reader agrees that under no circumstances is the author responsible for any losses, direct or indirect, that are incurred as a result of the use of the information contained within this document, including, but not limited to, errors, omissions, or inaccuracies.

Contents

Introduction 1
   Reading, Writing, and the Modern World 1
   What Can Plain English Do for You? 2
   Reaching the Most People 2
   How This Book Will Help 3

Chapter 1: Plain English: What, Why, and How? 5
   What Is Plain English? 5
   Why Use Plain English? 6
      Who Benefits From Plain English? 9
   How to Use Plain English 11
      Learning From Web Writing 13
   Key Takeaways 15

Chapter 2: Out With the Bad Text,
   In With the Good! 17
   What's a Good Text? 17
      Focus 17
      Development 18
      Unity 18
      Coherence 18
      Correctness 19
   What's a Bad Text? 19
      Vague, Unclear Writing 19
      Ignoring Your Readers 20
      Failure to edit 21
      Awkward Transitions 21
      Filler words 22
      Cliches 22
   Five Steps to a Good Text 23
      Consider Your Reader 23

Organize Your Information 24
Write Your Content 25
Check Your Work 26
Design and Produce... 26
Examples of Good and Bad Texts 27
Key Takeaways 29

Chapter 3: Grammar and Structure 31

Why Do You Need to Know Grammar?.. 31
Parts of Speech.. 32
Nouns and Pronouns 32
    Examples 33
Verbs 33
    Simple Tenses... 33
    Perfect Tense 34
Adjectives and Adverbs.. 34
    Adjectives 35
    Adverbs 35
Comparative Adjectives and Adverbs... 35
Word Order and Structure... 36
    Sentences With Only Subject and Verb................................. 36
    Sentences With Subject, Verb, and Direct Object 37
    Sentences With Subject, Verb, and Indirect Object 37
Tips and Tricks for Better Grammar and Structure.......... 37
    Avoid Double Negatives 37
    Avoid Weak Verbs if possible 37
    Avoid Weak Adjectives if possible.. 38
Effective Sentence Structure for Plain English 38
Basic Sentence Structure 39
    Simple Sentence 39
    Compound Sentence 39
    Complex Sentence 40
    Compound-Complex Sentence... 40
    Conditional Clauses.. 41

Paragraph Structure 41
    Poor Structure 42
    Better Structure 42
    Poor Structure 43
    Better Structure 43
    Poor Structure 43
    Better Structure 44
Writing Effective Sentences in Plain English 44
    Don't Combine Too Many Ideas 44
    Vary Your Sentence Structure 45
    Active and Passive Voice 46
Key Takeaways 47

Chapter 4: Capitalization and Punctuation 49

Capitalization 49
    Initial Capitals 50
    Title Case 51
    Acronyms 52
Punctuation 53
    Period 53
    Question Marks and Exclamation Points 54
    Comma 54
    Quotation Marks 55
    Apostrophe 55
    Parentheses and Dashes 56
    Hyphen 57
    Colon 57
    Semicolon 58
Key Takeaways 59

Chapter 5: Planning Your Writing 60

Consider Your Readers 60
    Who Is Your Target Audience? 60
    What Do Your Readers Need to Know? 61
The Importance of Layout 62
    White Space 63

    Headings and Subheadings 63
    Structure 64
    Color 64
    Images 65
Infographics 66
Planning the Look of Your Text 71
    Type 71
    Typefaces 71
    Type Size 72
    Type Style 72
    Spacing 73
    Alignment 73
Key Takeaways 74

Chapter 6: What to Avoid in Plain English Writing 76

Jargon 76
    Computer 77
    Business 78
    Legal Jargon 80
    Medical Jargon 82
Idioms 84
Nominalization 86
    Gerunds 86
    Noun Phrases 86
    Endings 87
Key Takeaways 88

Chapter 7: Review Your Writing 89

Editing Your Work 89
    Leave It Alone 89
    Read It Aloud 90
    Use a Focus Group 90
    Software Tools 91
    Professional Editing 92
The Editing Process 92
    Structural Editing 93

Copy Editing 93
Proofreading 94
House Style and Style Guide 95
Benefits of a Style Guide 96
Creating Your Style Guide 97
Checklist for a Plain English Style Guide 99
Key Takeaways 100

Chapter 8: Plain English Checklist and Templates 101

What's a Template? 101
Checklist 101
Business Emails 103
Tips for Writing Emails 103
The Formal Email 105
Formal Email Template 105
Informal Email 106
Informal Email Template 107
Business Letter 107
Example of a Business Letter 108
Business Letter Template 110
Business Memo 110
Business Memo 111
Discussion 111
Summary 111
Closing 111
Business Memo Example 112
Business Report 112
Example of Business Report 113
Template for Business Report 114

Conclusion 115
Glossary 118
About the Author 121
References 122

Introduction

Reading and writing are essentials in modern life. Writing with clarity and reading with understanding are skills that mean success for every business and also for every worker and every customer of that business.

So, why is so much writing hard to read? It's often crammed with difficult words and trendy jargon. Sentences and paragraphs seem to go on forever. The meaning gets lost and the reader feels defeated by how hard it is to understand.

You'd think that businesses would make it easy for people to understand their communications. Instead, many seem to feel that if a piece of writing is difficult, it proves that the writer is smart. What's really smart is writing in a way that builds bridges among employers, employees, clients, contractors and customers!

Reading, Writing, and the Modern World

The world has changed. Once, it was possible to communicate in the workplace by speaking in person or demonstrating a process. Even a person's body language and tone of voice conveyed information.

Now most communication is written. Websites, emails, business documents, employee handbooks, and more, require writing and reading skills to communicate with and to understand each other. More people than ever are working from home and not able to meet face-to-face with their coworkers or clients. Coworkers or clients could even be in different countries.

Wouldn't it be great to have a way to write so well that everyone could understand what you're trying to say? Well, there is a way, and it's called plain English. Using plain English will help businesses perform better, save time and money, help build an effective workforce, and increase customer satisfaction.

What Can Plain English Do for You?

Plain English is ideal for communication between managers and employees, employees and their coworkers, employees and contractors, and even teachers and students. Learning how to use the techniques of plain English benefits everyone.

Some businesses, governments, banks, and universities already use plain English for their communications because it's so necessary for people to understand their documents.

Plain English is helpful at home as well as at work. Think about all the things you read in a day, from words on the TV screen to social media, recipes, and magazines. Although many people get their news by listening to TV or podcasts, you can get a greater depth of information from written sources. Making written communication understandable has an impact on most parts of your life.

Reaching the Most People

Using plain English is especially helpful when you are communicating with someone who isn't a native English speaker. People who learn English as an Additional Language or Dialect (EALD) can be easily confused by writing that is too complicated and full of unfamiliar words. Misunderstandings can easily happen, leading to lost time and money—and even workplace accidents.

There are also many readers who have learning difficulties or have left school before graduating. People who can't read above a sixth-grade level are not "functionally literate," meaning they can't get enough information from what they read to get by in their daily lives. Writing in plain English will help them get that information more easily and improve their lives.

How This Book Will Help

How to Write in Plain English is a practical guide to effective communication. It includes examples that demonstrate the difference between good, effective documents and bad, confusing documents. We'll look at how to simplify language without "dumbing it down." We'll help you look at the documents you've already written and suggest ways to make your writing clear, helpful, and understandable.

Along the way, you'll learn about some of the rules of plain English grammar and sentence structure. You can use this information to make sure that your own writing tells your story the way you want and need it to. We'll cover what kinds of language to avoid when you want to make your meaning clear. And we'll give you some handy templates that will walk you through the process of producing common business documents.

If you equip yourself with the knowledge of plain English in this book, you can practice the skills you've gained until you are confident. You'll see an improvement in your ability to communicate clearly and effectively, making the most of the effort that you put into writing. You'll be setting yourself up for success, one effective word at a time!

CHAPTER 1

Plain English: What, Why, and How?

Everyone has had the experience of reading an email or a text—sometimes reading it more than once—and still not being able to figure out what it means. It's confusing and frustrating but it doesn't have to be that way!

Some people feel obligated to use complicated language and difficult words. People in management positions, doctors, lawyers, manufacturers, and other business professionals often write this way. If they knew that too-complex writing could cost a business money and time, they would be eager to find a way to simplify things.

Fortunately, there is a solution to the problem: plain English. Let's take a look.

What Is Plain English?

People have been looking for a way to simplify and clarify writing since at least the middle of the 1900s. Writers and readers noticed that the English language was more difficult to read than it needed to be. Highly technical language and specialized terms from unfamiliar professions made it hard to understand written communication—everything from novels to newspapers to advertising to business letters. Writer George Orwell, author of the novel *1984*, was one well-known Englishman who tried to spread the idea.

What did Orwell and others mean when they spoke about plain English? Plain English is speech or writing that is easy to understand, so the audience will get the message the first time they hear or read it. Plain English texts contain clear, concise language with no ambiguity. That way, readers have an easier time figuring out what is really being said. They won't have to reread the message several times to determine if they have missed anything.

Some people believe that concise, understandable writing means you have to "dumb down" texts, but that isn't what plain English is really all about. Plain English can be used for important topics or serious information in a way that makes them more accessible. People who use plain English believe that readers should be able to understand written texts that will help them get along in life. If writers use plain English, reading won't be such a chore.

In fact, some people believe that all government and business documents should be written in plain English. For example, lawmakers have been trying to simplify tax forms and instructions so that regular citizens, who represent many different languages and cultures, don't need an accountant to figure them out. Just as providing important documents and signs in Spanish, Arabic, or other languages enables more people to navigate daily life, plain English helps every English speaker get through their day more easily.

Why Use Plain English?

Life would be easier if more people and organizations used plain English. It's absolutely possible to present even difficult explanations simply. Even when the intended audience is the general public, plain English will help in making the writers' points clear.

Which would you rather read? This:

- *A matter of great importance has come to light in the past few days. All personnel are not abiding by the requirements for timely arrival at their place of work. Timeliness is paramount for the accomplishment of the organization's mission and for assuring that the customer experience proceeds in an efficient process. No personnel are exempt from fulfilling their duty to commence work by 9:00 a.m. Those employees who do not conform to this standard will face consequences including reprimands if the offense is repeated.*

Or this:

- *Opening on time is very important to our business and our customers. All employees must arrive at work by 9:00 a.m; recently, some employees have been arriving after 9:00 a.m. You must be in the workplace by 9:00 a.m., or the company will write you up. If the company writes you up more than three times, you will receive a warning.*

The second statement is shorter, and it's also easier to understand. A memo or email like the first one can be confusing, especially for readers who don't understand English well. About 1.35 billion of the world's people can speak English, but most of them aren't native speakers (Lyons, 2021). Many are fluent in another language, but less comfortable using English. Unfamiliar words and complex sentence structures can be confusing for them. People who have English as an Additional Language or Dialect (EALD) can often struggle to interpret wordy instructions and they tend to lose track of what they're reading. By the time they finish reading a sentence or paragraph, they may have forgotten what the beginning was about.

Even adults whose first language is English can struggle with written communication. In the US, 21% of adults cannot read or write at all, and another 54% can't read at higher than a sixth-grade level (48+ US Literacy Statistics, 2022). Despite this, most government documents are written at a ninth-grade level.

In Canada, where English is the most-spoken language, around 16% of people can't read or write well enough to meet their ordinary, basic needs, and 40% are considered to have low literacy. The benefits of literacy are many: "Canadians with higher literacy skills earn more income, are more likely to have full-time work, are less likely to be unemployed, and spend shorter periods of time unemployed" (Bailey, et al., 2013).

Adult Literacy in 4 English-Speaking Countries: Percentage of Adults at Year 6 Literacy Level (12 year-old level) or Lower

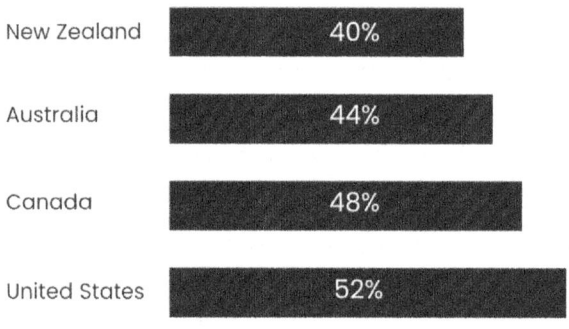

Foster (2022)

Who Benefits From Plain English?

As noted, many adults are not able to read a lot of the writing they encounter because they read at the elementary school level. They aren't able to understand long, complicated sentences or documents that don't quickly say what they mean. It will be easier for these people to understand information that is presented in plain English.

However, plain English can also benefit highly educated readers, who may struggle with the unfamiliar wording and complicated sentence structure found in healthcare and legal documents.

For example, professors in college can use plain English to make course requirements easier to follow. Students can use it to make any papers they write more understandable. People applying for jobs can write better resumes and application letters in plain English. Marketers can make their ads more powerful by getting to the important facts first and by avoiding slang or idioms that non-native English speakers may not be familiar with.

The most important place to use plain English is in the world of business. Using plain language can give you an edge over your competitors—it will show potential and existing customers that you really care about their needs, and that you want to help them understand your products or services. It will also be easier for them to remember your message.

Using plain English can save your business time. If customers don't understand your communications, you'll likely receive unnecessary phone calls, emails, and complaints. Customers may even return your products if they can't figure out how to use them based on unclear instructions. Responding to these situations will cost you time, money, and good will.

The healthcare field, especially, can benefit from using plain English. If healthcare providers communicate in plain English, they can prevent mistakes, even expensive or potentially deadly ones. Plain English makes it less likely that patients will end up taking incorrect dosages of medicine. They're also more likely to understand all their doctor's healthcare instructions, which will benefit them in the long term.

Too many medical documents look like this:

- *Having statistically higher than normal results on various tests, patient is considered to be hypertensive and hyperglycemic. Precautionary measures to prevent undesirable outcomes include regular monitoring of blood values; adjustment of diet to include lower sodium and sugars; and adherence to a regimen of medications which will alleviate the symptoms. Re-evaluation on a quarterly basis is recommended.*

Isn't it better when a doctor reports this to their patients?

- *Your tests show that you have high blood pressure and high blood sugar. Avoid foods that are high in salt. You should try to eat less food that is high in salt or sugar. There are drugs that can help, too, if you take them regularly. Come back in three months so we can check your progress.*

Other industries, such as the legal profession, marketing, as well as manufacturing, can benefit from the use of plain language. Plain English in the manufacturing industry can help employees understand instructions better and help avoid accidents that occur as a result of not understanding clearly what they're supposed to do.

How to Use Plain English

There are a number of techniques that can help you write in plain English, which will let you present information in an understandable way for your readers. We'll cover the details in future chapters, but here are a few of the basics.

Think about what you want to say and try to write the information in clear, logical, short sentences and paragraphs. The average sentence length should be 15 to 20 words (the first sentence in this paragraph is 20 words long). Not all sentences should be the same length. Sentences of all one length sound flat, boring, and too simplistic. Look at this paragraph:

- *All sentences should be seven words long. More words than that can be confusing. You want your writing to be clear. You don't want to use confusing words. Plain English will help you write clearly.*

Now look at this one:

- *Plain English sentences can be any length. Even though long sentences can be confusing, they don't have to be. You can still write clearly without making your writing sound short and choppy. Readers will be glad you did.*

The second example paragraph has sentences that are from six to thirteen words long. It flows better and is still understandable. It doesn't sound like a simple reader for primary school students. Try to keep sentences to one main idea, adding a related point if you need to (like this one does).

Information that is not essential to your readers can be left out. The most important topic or information should appear in the first sentence of a paragraph. The connections within paragraphs should also be clear. You can achieve this by using transition words such as "also," "for example," and "in addition." Here's an example.

> - *Scheduling your time is an important way to make your business successful. You've heard the saying, "Time is money," which means that making good use of time will also save you money. For example, a good schedule can keep you from wasting time on unimportant tasks. Instead, you could be doing things that actually make you money.*

The first sentence tells what the paragraph will be about—the most important information. The rest of the sentences offer reasons that the opening sentence is important. The words "for example" and "instead" make connections between the ideas.

Another important way to help readers connect to your text is by addressing the reader directly, using pronouns like "you" and "we." For example, "You can learn to schedule your time" or "We'll go over the reasons next." If you have something negative to say, it may be better not to use pronouns but instead to say something like "Many people don't read entire books."

There are other ways to make your plain English sentences and paragraphs easier to read, and we'll introduce them in the upcoming chapters. Now, we're going to show you how the modern process of writing for websites can improve many kinds of writing.

Learning From Web Writing

While short paragraphs and sentences can make your documents more readable, design features can also make your documents easier to understand and read. These features are usually part of writing for the web, which can teach us a lot about plain English.

Common forms of writing on the web include news reports, ads, blogs, and social media posts. People who write these kinds of communications use many of the principles of plain English writing. Web writing may be a little different from other types of writing, but many of its features can be useful for producing any documents in plain English.

Web writing is almost like having a conversation with someone, so it's too informal for academic writing and some forms of business communication. However, a clear and relatable voice can be used to interact with customers and coworkers in most forms of business writing. You can learn from the layout of web pages, blogs, etc., because they are usually set up to help people find the information they need as quickly as possible.

Think about an ad for a product that you might see on the web. It's likely to have a headline, then a sentence or two explaining what the product is. Next, you'll see a smaller heading with a bulleted list of the features of the product—what it does or why it's the best product for the job. It might look like this:

Make Your Home Cleaner With the Super-Sweeper!

This powerful tool will cut down on the time you spend sweeping and mopping, letting you have more time for more enjoyable activities.

The All-New Super-Sweeper

- Quick and easy to use
- Patented high-tech motor
- New, sturdier design

The first headline tells the reader what the product is and what it does, just as the first sentences of a paragraph tell what it's going to be about: in this case, that the product is a cleaning tool. The text underneath the heading tells a little more about the product, like the sentences in a paragraph do for the topic.

Next, you'll see a "subhead," in this case, "The All-New Super-Sweeper." It's like the headline, only smaller in size and usually shorter. Then comes a bulleted list of the features of the product. These do not have to be full sentences, but should give important information.

You might use these same types of writing in a blog post, for example, or a poster telling about an employee picnic. It might look like this:

Employee Picnic This Saturday

Come gather with your friends and meet your coworkers at Waterside Park at 3:00! There will be two hours of fun and food for the whole family.

Games and Prizes

- Volleyball
- Softball
- Trivia Contest

You can also use headings to break up texts like reports, blog posts, and even emails. Headings will help your readers find relevant information faster, because they tell readers what the text is about. That way, they can tell which parts are most important to them.

Key Takeaways

- Some people use complicated English words and, which can cause challenges when it comes to business and other communication. If you use plain English, your readers will understand your message the first time.
- Plain English simply involves the use of clear, straightforward language and doesn't mean that texts have to be "dumbed down." Plain English is suitable for any reader, from the general public to people in specialized businesses and even government.
- Using levels of English that are too difficult for some people to understand can have serious consequences. For example, patients may take an incorrect dose of their medication if they don't understand the medicine label.
- Using plain English can save your business time and work when it comes to minimizing questions and complaints.
- It will be easier for your customers to remember your message if it's in plain English.
- The clear and relatable voice of web writing can be used when writing in plain English. Just be aware that web-style writing might be too informal for academic papers and some types of business communication.

- Design elements such as headings, subheadings, and bulleted lists can also play an important role when it comes to creating documents in plain English.

CHAPTER 2

Out With the Bad Text, In With the Good!

Knowing the differences between a well-written text and a badly written one is a good step toward producing well-written documents. A well-written document is clear, logical, organized, and easy to read and understand. A badly written document is often vague and full of filler words and cliches, which make the meaning of the document unclear. Plain English will help you produce well-written texts and avoid badly written ones.

What's a Good Text?

First, we're going to consider the characteristics of a well-written plain language English text. Keep these in mind when you start to write a document.

Focus

A well-written piece of text is focused. It quickly gets to the main idea and doesn't allow unrelated information in a sentence, paragraph, or document. For example, if you are writing a notice about a new company policy for requesting days off for a vacation, you should stick to that topic and not include information on a different policy, such as days off for holidays or illness.

A good subject line will help both you and your readers focus on the topic. For the vacation policy, a bad one would be "On Requesting Time Off When You Want to Take a Vacation." It's too long and hard to follow. "New Policy on Vacation

Requests" is better. It emphasizes that the information is new and says what the new policy is for.

Development

Development refers to the way you support a topic—it's about giving more information about it. A procedure or list of instructions is a simple way to develop a topic. You can use a numbered list for the steps in the process, which will take the reader through it. Development on an email about an updated employee handbook might start with how long it's been since the old manual came out, then move to why you've decided to issue a new one. Finally, you should list the changes and maybe an explanation of why each one was made.

Development makes a topic more understandable because it provides clear reasons for an action or situation.

Unity

Unity means sticking to a topic once you introduce it. All the paragraphs and sentences should be about the same main topic. They can offer more information on the same topic, but shouldn't wander off to other topics. These side topics can be discussed in a separate document, or under a different subheading.

When you write a text with unity, the readers will understand the topic better because everything in the document relates to the same idea. Rambling, disconnected ideas are confusing.

Coherence

Coherence is another important part of good plain English writing. A reader should be able to follow the writer's thought process through the entire text. Coherence prevents confusion and misunderstandings.

A piece of writing is coherent when it moves through the information in a logical manner. For example, the steps of a process should come in order, not skip around it. A coherent paragraph starts with a major idea, then supports it with evidence such as facts, informed opinions, history, logic, definitions, and/or explanations. The ideas presented should support, not contradict, each other.

Correctness

The characteristic of good writing that most people think of is correctness. You may think of correctness as meaning grammar, sentence structure, and punctuation—and those are important. But we'll be covering them in future chapters.

Correctness also means that any facts and figures you use to support your main idea are true and accurate. Any quotations you use should be exactly what the person said. You may have to do research to make sure that everything in a document is correct. That's part of the writing process.

What's a Bad Text?

Just as there are qualities that make up a well-written plain English text, there are also characteristics that tell you a text is badly written. Naturally, you want to avoid them when you write. Here are some to watch out for.

Vague, Unclear Writing

Writing that is vague and unclear is difficult to understand. Vague writing is the opposite of specific, clear writing. It doesn't get to the point right away or describes ideas in very general terms. Vague writing often contains words like "kind of," "sort of," or "maybe." The information in a paragraph doesn't support the main idea, but rather brings in other topics that should be explained in paragraphs of their own—or left out entirely.

"The product leaflet needs to be improved" by itself is vague. It doesn't say *how* the leaflet can be made better. "The product brochure needs to be shorter and more appealing visually" is much clearer. Then the paragraph or email can go on to talk about ways to make the brochure shorter and what will give it more visual impact.

Ignoring Your Readers

Knowing who will be reading your writing is important for choosing what and how to write. Are your readers familiar with a technical topic like computers? If not, you may have to explain terms thoroughly, rather than using abbreviations. Are your readers busy professionals? They may prefer writing that gets to the point quickly. Do your readers speak English as a second language? You won't want to use complicated sentence structures or difficult words. Are they customers? Prospective employees? Vendors? How you write will depend on who you need to communicate with.

If you're writing a document for the general public, it's best to assume your audience is intelligent, but may not be familiar with your topic. Before you write, ask yourself what your reader might need from your communication—instructions, explanations, facts, advertising copy, or a report, for example. Consider questions that your readers may need to have answered and then create your document to do this.

People like to read writing that is targeted to them specifically. Think about your ideal reader. That might be someone who is looking for a product they want to buy. Writing for that reader should be upbeat and informative. They won't want long, involved explanations. A reader who needs to know how to fill out a form will appreciate writing that is straightforward and practical.

Failure to edit

Failing to edit your work means that you may send out incorrect information or text that is difficult to read and understand.

Editing your work is one of the most important steps in writing. To edit, you look over your writing before you send or publish it. You make sure that you have included all the information your reader needs, and that it is presented in the right order. If not, you need to make changes.

When you're editing, you also want to look at the characteristics of your writing. We've just discussed what the characteristics of good writing are. Make sure your writing takes advantage of them. Are your sentences varied in length but not too long? Do your paragraphs contain one main idea each?

Awkward Transitions

Transitions help connect your sentences and paragraphs to each other. Your writing should flow together smoothly. Good transitions will help that happen, while awkward transitions will make your writing sound choppy and disconnected.

Transitions often include words like "instead," "for example," "rather than," or "therefore." The simple words "and," "but," and "or" can help you make smooth transitions too.

Here are sentences that have awkward transitions.

- Don't use general terms when you talk to customers. They may not understand. Use precise language. Don't say only that we have a customer service department. Tell them that they can return a purchase at the information desk. They need to have a receipt.

Now, let's look at smoother transitions that connect the ideas.

- Use precise language rather than general terms when you speak to customers, so they will understand better. For example, when a customer needs help, don't just tell them that we have a customer service department. Instead, tell them that to return a purchase, they can take their receipt to the information desk.

Filler words

Filler words are ones that add nothing to a sentence, but merely take up space. "There is" and "there are" are common filler words. Instead of saying "There are a lot of people who live by the lake," say simply, "A lot of people live by the lake." You can even make the sentence shorter and more direct by getting rid of "a lot of people" and saying, "Many people."

You can make your sentences shorter by removing repeated words. Words that do not add anything to the meaning of a sentence can also be left out. For example, "Take the train in order to get to the office" could simply be "Take the train to get to the office." "Lisa has the ability to read a spreadsheet" could be rewritten as "Lisa can read a spreadsheet."

Cliches

Cliches are expressions that used to be clever and meaningful once, but are now trite and unimaginative. Examples of cliches are "think outside the box," or "you can't judge a book by its cover." Cliches can be a shorthand way of saying something, but more often they are dull, hard to understand and overused.

They make writing less interesting and are therefore less likely to engage the reader.

You'll have the same effect if you say, "Contribute some fresh, new ideas" or "Don't make decisions based on first impressions." They're less boring. When people are too familiar with cliches or don't understand them, they tend to read right over them.

Five Steps to a Good Text

Writing good plain English text is easier if you follow the following procedure: Consider your reader. Organize your information. Write your content. Check your writing. Design and produce the document.

Consider Your Reader

We've already discussed thinking about your reader's needs—their first language and education level, and knowledge of technical terms, for example. But there are other things to consider as well.

Addressing your readers directly by using pronouns like "you" and "we," is more likely to focus their attention on themselves. The pronoun "they" should be used sparingly. Readers may not be sure whether the sentence applies to them. For example, "We'll have an important fire drill tomorrow" or "You need to take fire drills seriously" are better than "People need to pay attention to fire drills. They need to know what to do in case of an emergency."

Readers respond better to information that is communicated in a positive tone of voice. They're likely to receive your message better. Your meaning will also be clearer to your audience, as positive statements are more direct and concise.

For example, "The project will not be finished until Friday" is phrased negatively. "The project will be finished on Friday" is more positive and also clearer.

You can also boost the positive tone of your document by leaving out negative details that may not be relevant to your audience. For example, your business may be struggling, but your employees don't need to know all the details. In your communication or on your internal website, simply state that your business is working towards achieving better growth over the next year.

Also, think how you want your readers to respond. Do you want them to buy a product? Complete a project? Learn how to change spark plugs? Each of these goals will require a different approach to writing. Sales writing is intended to convince the reader to make a purchase. An email to team members can motivate them to work harder. Instructions require steps in the proper sequence.

Organize Your Information

Gather the information you need for your piece of writing in one place so you don't have to go racing all over to find it once you've started writing. If you're working online, create a separate tab for each resource so you can flip back and forth between them. Select your writing tool: Word, PowerPoint, Adobe, or another piece of software.

Create an outline. This doesn't have to be the kind of formal outline that you may be used to from high school days. You can set it up in your online writing tool or even handwritten on a legal pad.

Decide what will be the main message of the document. Write this message in a simple sentence of not more than 20 words.

Place the main message at the beginning of the document, so that readers can decide early on if they need to read the document. You may want to use this sentence in the introduction to the piece of writing or the topic of the first paragraph.

Then, write a sentence for the topic of each of the following paragraphs. Record them on your outline. Leave space between the sentences—that's where you'll make notes on your supporting elements such as facts and figures or instructions.

Your outline may change as you incorporate your research. You may realize that one main idea is more important than another and decide to swap the order of them. You could discover that a supporting idea isn't really necessary and eliminate it.

Write Your Content

You can use your outline to shape the content that you write. Make each heading a separate paragraph—or two, if the paragraph is getting too long. Keep an eye on how long each sentence is and whether you have filler words or cliches in them. Make sure you have transitions between sentences and paragraphs to help your readers follow what you are saying.

Make use of your word processing program's tools. Some have a grammar checker that will pinpoint problems. Most of them have a word count feature, a spelling checker, a way to make bold headings, and a way to choose your font (typeface) and spacing between lines. If you are unsure about this, you can use a template or checklist—more about this in Chapter 8.

You don't have to write your document all at one sitting. It may be better to take a break, do something else, and come back to your writing with fresh eyes and a clear head. Maybe work on a paragraph or two at a time, then get up and walk around. It will also help if you schedule your writing for a time when you don't have frequent interruptions that will derail your train of thought.

Check Your Work

Before you send that email or print out your report, you need to proofread and edit your work. Take your outline and compare it to the finished text. Have you left out anything? Have you thought of something new you should add? Now is the time to fix it. If you have someone on staff who has a good knowledge of grammar and punctuation, they would be a good choice.

Have another person read through your document so they can make sure that it does what you need it to and to notice any mistakes. Afterward, ask if your test reader understands what the text says. If any part is confusing to them, the intended audience will be likely to misunderstand it too.

Before you print your document or hit send, read through it one more time, slowly. One trick that proofreaders and editors use is to read the document out loud. This makes you look at every word and will help you notice a missing word, for example. If you are in the office and can't read out loud, use the 'read aloud' function on your software program. You might need your headphones on for this.

Design and Produce

If you notice your document consists of long paragraphs of text that makes it hard to read, you may need to make the layout more reader-friendly. You can insert bold subheadings to make it easier for readers to find their way through the content. You could consider making a subheading a complete sentence that tells the main point of the section. For instance, if you have a section about how invoices are processed, you could have a subheading that says, "Invoices will be processed on the 15th and 30th of the month." The rest of the section could say who is responsible for processing the invoices and what the deadline is for turning them in.

If you're producing an advertisement, you want to make sure it's reader-friendly. It should contain elements like a catchy headline that draws the reader in, a clear description of the product or service you're offering, and a call to action—how to purchase the product, when and where the seminar is going to be held, etc. You may want to have a graphic element on the ad that says how long a sale will last or how much of a discount you're offering.

Make sure the type is large enough for the audience to read and the graphics are well-placed. Pay attention to colors, too. For example, reading white type on a light blue background is difficult; a red background might be a better choice.

Think about how you are going to distribute your document. Would it be better to send it out as an email or pass out paper copies of it in a meeting? Does your printer have the capacity to make all the copies you'll need? If not, you should plan for a visit to a local print shop.

Examples of Good and Bad Texts

Take a look at these bad texts. Can you see what's wrong with them? Too wordy? Too confusing? Then look at the good versions of the same information. What's different?

Bad

Frequently, tools and other such equipment can be compromised when they have not been inspected carefully for signs of degradation of condition along with said tools having unsafe surfaces, namely rust. You are expected to perform this inspection every week to ensure that you are in compliance with our safety protocols. Notification to management of any deficiencies is required immediately so that necessary amelioration can be made. Be vigilant about following this set of instructions and about ensuring that all safety procedures are implemented.

Good

Your tools and equipment must be checked for safety.

- Inspect tools and equipment weekly to make sure they're in good condition.
- Always check for rust.
- Tell management about any problems you find.

Bad

It is most imperative for an adequately stocked first aid kit to be set aside in a suitable area with high traffic so that should its use be required, one can locate it without bother. An employee of high standing should have gone through a training process and be the first point of call in any incident to apply their first aid skill.

Good

A first aid kit will be located in a convenient location. An employee will soon be trained in first aid—contact this employee if you or anyone else requires first aid.

Bad

This email is to let you know that our company has experienced a downturn in business and will not be able to pay your invoice as scheduled on May 30th. We will inform you of the time when we will be able to pay it, so your bookkeeping department will know what we will be able to do and when we will be able to do it.

Good

We want to let you know that our payment will be late this month. We'll keep you informed of when we will send the payment or a partial payment.

Key Takeaways

- If you know the characteristics of well-written plain English, you can write or rewrite complex documents into plain English.
- A badly written document is often vague and full of unnecessary words and cliches.
- Short, simple words are good for most audiences, as not everyone will understand industry jargon or complicated words and sentences.
- Your communication will be better received if it has a positive tone.
- Before you create a document, consider your readers' needs. What information should they get from your document?
- Addressing your readers directly will make sure that they're more engaged with your document.

- Have one main idea for each section and each paragraph.

In Chapter 3, we will consider grammar, style, and sentence structure.

CHAPTER 3

Grammar and Structure

Good grammar is important because it provides information that can help you get your message across. Sentence structure conveys precise meaning from the writer to the audience. If you know the rules of the language, it will be easier for you to produce documents in plain English. Using correct grammar and sentence structure will make it more likely that readers will stay engaged with your message. Reduce grammatical errors from your writing, and reward your readers with clearer communication!

Why Do You Need to Know Grammar?

While many people regard grammar as boring and difficult, you need to understand the basics to get your message across successfully. This is especially important if you're trying to simplify your communication with plain English. Too much deviation from grammar rules can cause your reader difficulties, and your audience could struggle to understand your meaning. Good grammar can build a bridge between you and your audience.

Here are some important elements of grammar you need to be able to create meaning. Without these basics, it will be difficult to write messages that any audience can understand.

Parts of Speech

There are different types of words you will use in writing plain English. The most important ones are nouns and verbs. Other parts of speech include prepositions, adjectives, and adverbs.

Nouns and Pronouns

Nouns name a person, place, or thing. Some examples are assistant, office, or desk. Nouns can also be ideas, or things you can't touch. Courage, dreams, and pride are all nouns.

Pronouns take the place of nouns in a sentence. The pronouns are I, me, mine, myself; you, your, yours, yourself; he, his, himself; she, her, hers, herself; they, them, their, themselves, depending on what part they play in a sentence.

- *She* wrote the report.
- *Her* report was interesting.
- The report was *hers*.
- She wrote the report *herself*.

If we didn't have pronouns, we would end up with sentences like: Yoshi printed a copy of Yoshi's document for the committee and for Yoshi. It would be repetitive and hard to understand. It's much clearer if you say: Yoshi printed a copy of his document for the committee and for himself.

Recently, there have been changes in how personal pronouns are used. Some people prefer to use pronouns other than the usual ones. For example, a person may choose to use the pronoun "they" rather than "he" or "she." It is polite to use the pronouns that a person prefers. Many people sign emails with their preferred pronouns or indicate which pronouns they use in the heading.

Examples

- Amanda Quint (she/her)
- Rhonda Hooper (they/their)
- Matt Maguire (they/their)

Verbs

Verbs are usually words that express actions. Some verbs are "give," "receive," "play," "eat," and "work." They have tenses, or ways to show when the action happened. There are more complicated tenses such as the future tense and the past perfect tense. For now, we'll concentrate on the easier ones.

The present tense is just the verb itself or the verb with -s added to it—work becomes works; and play becomes plays. for example. The regular past tense is made by taking the verb and adding -d or -ed to it like this: received, played. The future tense is used for something that hasn't happened yet. It is formed by adding *will* before the verb. The present, past, and future tenses are called the "simple tenses."

Simple Tenses

- Roger *works* in the Cincinnati office. He *worked* in the Boston office last year. He *will work* in the Atlanta office next year.
- Kelly *receives* 20 emails every day. Yesterday, she *received* 25. Tomorrow, she *will receive* more than usual.

There are verbs that don't follow this pattern. They are called *irregular* verbs. Irregular verbs aren't formed by adding the endings -s, -es, -d, or -ed. "To be" is the most often used irregular verb. The present tense of "to be" looks like this: I *am*, he or she *is*, they or you *are*. The past tense would be: You or they *were*; I, he, or she *was*. Other irregular verbs are mostly short, simple ones—eat, give, write, for example. The past tense of these example words are *ate*, *gave*, and *wrote*.

Unfortunately, since irregular verbs don't follow a pattern, you simply have to memorize them. Fortunately, there are many more regular verbs than irregular ones. But it's important to know the irregular verbs and use them correctly. Since the irregular verbs are so short and common, they are used a lot in all kinds of speaking and writing.

Verbs can also have other, more complex tenses that use "helping verbs" such as *have, been,* and *are*. These are called the "perfect tenses," and they are more difficult to understand. In grammar "perfect" means "before". If this tense is confusing for you, use it as little as possible. Stick to the simple tenses whenever you can.

Perfect Tense

- I *will have been reading* for two hours at 3:00.
- Jackson *had read* the memo, but he didn't understand it.

Adjectives and Adverbs

Adjectives and adverbs are describing words. Adjectives describe nouns, and adverbs describe verbs. They tell what something looks like or acts like. There can be more than one adjective or adverb in a sentence. Many adverbs are formed by adding -ly to another word such as a noun or an adjective. Adjectives usually go before the noun they describe, and adverbs usually come after the verb they describe.

Adjectives

- The *weak* fence collapsed.
- Marisol wrote a *long, detailed* report.

Adverbs

- Marisol wrote her report *quickly*.
- The fence collapsed *suddenly* and *noisily*.

Comparative Adjectives and Adverbs

Comparative adjectives and adverbs are just what they sound like—ways to compare what something is like. Both comparative adjectives and comparative adverbs are formed by adding -er to the basic adjective and often use the words "than" "more" or "less". Superlatives are formed by adding -est to the basic adjective and use the words "most" or "least". Sometimes you have to double the final consonant. With adverbs, change "y" to an "i" before you add the ending.

- high, higher, highest
- big, bigger, biggest
- early, earlier, earliest

Let's look at these sentences using the above comparatives and superlatives.

- Carissa starts work earlier than Justin (comparative – comparing two people.)

- Lina starts work the earliest out of the whole department (superlative – comparing more than two people.)

There's an exception to this (of course!), and that's the word "good." The comparative and superlative versions of this adjective are "better" and "best." The adverb form of "good" is "well," and it does not have comparative forms.

- Eva is a *good* speaker.
- Eva speaks *well*.

Word Order and Structure

English has basic rules for word order in sentences. The basic sentence structure in most European languages as well as English is subject + verb. If the sentence has an object, it goes after the verb. The subject should always be before the verb, and the object, if there is one, goes after the verb. This is called SVO word order. Most English sentences conform to this rule.

There are two different kinds of objects. Direct objects are ones that come immediately after the verb and can finish a sentence by themselves. Direct objects are nouns or pronouns that the verb does something to. Indirect objects tell who receives the noun in the sentence.

Sentences With Only Subject and Verb

- The manager owes.
- Susan writes.
- Ed teaches.

Sentences With Subject, Verb, and Direct Object

- The manager owes *money*.
- Susan writes *letters*.
- Ed teaches *grammar*.

Sentences With Subject, Verb, and Indirect Object

- The manager owes *his assistant* money.
- Susan writes *Luis* letters.
- Ed teaches *Daniel* grammar.

Tips and Tricks for Better Grammar and Structure

Avoid Double Negatives

Double negatives are incorrect because English allows only one negative word, such as *can't, won't, not, no,* or *never*, in a sentence. Using two negatives in a sentence will make your writing unclear and will sound wrong to most English-speakers. You can correct this by changing or eliminating one of the negative words.

- **Wrong**: I *can't* do *no* more work.
- **Right:** I can't do any more work.
- **Wrong:** I *never* got *none* of those orders.
- **Right:** I never got those orders.

Avoid Weak Verbs if possible

Weak verbs are ones that are ordinary and not very specific. Stronger verbs convey a more precise meaning that tells more about what is being done. If you tend to use weak verbs, replace them with more powerful verbs.

- **Weak:** I *walked* to the coffee shop.

- **Stronger:** I *strolled* to the coffee shop.
- **Weak:** She knows that he *loves* her.
- **Stronger:** She knows he *adores* her.
- **Weak:** Dan *tells* us about procedures.
- **Stronger:** Dan *informs* us about procedures.

Avoid Weak Adjectives if possible

Weak adjectives are like weak verbs. They don't describe things clearly and aren't very interesting. Weak adjectives often follow words like "very" and "really."

You can eliminate these by using stronger alternatives.

- **Weak:** Giselle was *very angry*.
- **Stronger:** Giselle was *furious*.
- **Weak:** Our success is due to your *really good* work.
- **Stronger:** Our success is due to your *exceptional* work.
- **Weak:** There is a *very large* pile of papers on my desk.
- **Stronger:** There is a *huge* pile of papers on my desk.

Effective Sentence Structure for Plain English

You want your readers to be able to read and understand your writing as quickly as possible. Plain English writing has a straightforward sentence structure, which will help your audience understand and remember your information better. Your writing shouldn't be open to misinterpretation.

Basic Sentence Structure

There are four types of sentences that you will mostly use in business writing. If you haven't majored in English, it's a good idea to review this point of grammar, as it will help you write more understandable sentences.

Simple Sentence

The simple sentence consists of one independent clause. An independent clause expresses a complete thought. It has a subject (noun performing the action), predicate (verb or action) and sometimes an object (noun that the action is done to). It is a complete thought.

- Suzy writes a memo.

"Suzy" is the noun, "writes" is the verb and "memo" is the object.

- Benjamin takes a vacation.

Compound Sentence

A compound sentence combines two or more independent clauses by using conjunctions. Each clause needs to have both a subject and a verb. A good way to remember the conjunctions is to spell out the word **FANBOYS**. These letters represent the 7 conjunctions—for, and, nor, but, or, yet, so.

- Ewan was at school, and James was at home.
- James was reading, but his mother was working.
- She was tired, yet she worked through the night.

Complex Sentence

These are sentences that consist of an independent clause and a dependent clause, or an incomplete thought. These incomplete thoughts can't stand on their own and need to be attached to independent clauses.

- She stopped studying because she was tired.

"Because she was tired" is the dependent clause. It isn't a sentence on its own.

- If she is such a good writer, why didn't she get the job?

"If she is such a good writer" is the dependent clause. It isn't a full sentence on its own.

Compound-Complex Sentence

Compound-complex sentences have at least two independent clauses and one or more dependent clauses. You won't use these sentences very often because they are usually long and complicated.

- Since she was sick, Michelle had to stay in bed, and she couldn't complete her assignment.

"Since she was sick" is the dependent clause. It can't be a sentence on its own. "Michelle had to stay in bed" and "she couldn't complete her assignment" are independent clauses. Either of them could be a sentence on its own.

- When my car broke down, I decided to walk home from the shop, and I couldn't buy everything I intended to, because it would be too heavy to carry home.

"When my car broke down" is a dependent clause, and so is "because it would be too heavy to carry home." Neither of them can be a sentence on its own. "I couldn't buy everything I intended to" is an independent clause. It could be a sentence on its own.

Conditional Clauses

In addition to independent and dependent clauses, there is another kind—the conditional clause. These are easily recognized because they use the word "if." These are dependent clauses, so they require a comma before or after the independent clause.

- If you meet your sales goals, you will receive a bonus.
- If Margaret calls today, tell her I'm not in.
- I want to speak to you this afternoon, if you're not busy.

Paragraph Structure

Just as there are several kinds of sentence structure, there are also many types of paragraph structure. However, there is one type of paragraph structure that is the most useful as well as the most common. Here's how it works.

The first sentence in the paragraph is the topic sentence or main idea. The other sentences in the paragraph support, explain, or expand on the main idea. There are a number of ways to organize these supporting sentences. They can be ordered or numbered—first, second, third, and so on. They can be put in order of importance, from most important to least important. You can even put the most important supporting point last, so that the paragraph ends on a strong note.

This is the same sort of structure that your entire document will have. The first paragraph of a document will set out the major point of the text. The following paragraphs will support or explain the first paragraph and be introduced in numerical order or order of importance.

Each paragraph needs smooth transitions within it to lead readers through the topic and the supporting sentences. You may also want the final sentence of a paragraph to lead into the next paragraph, if there is one. Like sentences, paragraphs can contain too many ideas. Put the extra ideas into a separate paragraph.

Here are some examples of a poorly structured paragraph and how it can be improved by proper structure. The actual sentences remain the same, but the order they appear in is different.

Poor Structure

From now on, anyone who is absent from work on Friday or Monday will need to have a doctor's note or take the day as a vacation day. We have decided that the absentee policy needs to be updated. If you have any questions about this policy, please contact the Human Resources Department. This is intended to ensure that we will be fully staffed both before and after the weekend. Of course, if Friday or Monday is a federal holiday, no doctor's note will be required.

Better Structure

We have decided that the absentee policy needs to be updated. From now on, anyone who is absent from work on Friday or Monday will need to have a doctor's note or take the day as a vacation day. This will ensure that we will be fully staffed both before and after the weekend. Of course, if Friday or Monday is a federal holiday, no doctor's note will be required. If you have any questions about this policy, please contact the Human Resources Department.

Poor Structure

Avoid highly technical terms, and make sure that any unfamiliar terms are defined when they first appear. The structure should include sentences of different lengths. If you want to write effective paragraphs in plain English, you will want to ensure that your structure and word choices are appropriate. You can check the length of your sentences by using a function in your word processing program. The sentences can be a mixture of simple, compound, complex, and complex sentences. A good average length for a sentence is 15 to 20 words. The words that make up those sentences should be ones that are easily understood by laypeople.

Better Structure

If you want to write effective paragraphs in plain English, you will want to ensure that your structure and word choices are appropriate. The structure should include sentences of different lengths; a good average length for a sentence is 15 to 20 words. You can check the length of your sentences by using a function in your word processing program. The sentences can be a mixture of simple, compound, complex, and complex sentences. The words that make up those sentences should be easily understood by laypeople. Avoid highly technical terms, and make sure that you define any unfamiliar terms when they first appear.

Poor Structure

All requests for vacation days should be submitted two weeks in advance. Vacation days will not be approved during the holiday season. If you are required to work on a federal holiday, you will receive time-and-a-half pay or another day off. When you call in sick, please give 12 hours notice. If you do not call in sick in a timely manner, you will receive a letter of reprimand. "Mental health" days are considered to be part of vacation time. You will receive two weeks of vacation after working here for five years.

Better Structure

You will receive two weeks of vacation after working here for five years. You should submit all requests for vacation days two weeks in advance. Vacation days will not be approved during the holiday season. If you need to work on a federal holiday, you will receive time-and-a-half pay or another day off. "Mental health" days are part of vacation time. When you call in sick, please give 12 hours notice if possible.

Writing Effective Sentences in Plain English

You need to keep a few basic rules in mind when you're doing business writing. You want to ensure that your writing is as easy as possible to understand in order to get your message across.

Don't Combine Too Many Ideas

You shouldn't combine too many ideas in one sentence or one paragraph. The text becomes confusing and difficult to read. One or maybe two ideas per sentence or paragraph is enough.

- **Too many ideas:** Lucy wrote the report, and the graphics were designed, and the document looked wonderful.

- **Fewer ideas:** Lucy wrote the report, while the design team produced the graphics. The final document looked wonderful.

Vary Your Sentence Structure

While it's good to write clear and simple sentences, you also have to vary your sentence structure, to make sure your readers won't stop reading because they're bored. Combining information can be easier to read than short, choppy sentences:

- **Choppy:** We are pleased. The company is doing well. We made a profit. Our earnings increased by five percent. Employees received bonuses at the end of the year.
- **Better:** We are pleased that the company is doing well and that we have made a profit. Because our earnings increased by five percent, employees received bonuses at the end of the year.

Texts with varying sentence structure are much easier to read. Use sentences of different lengths or a combination of simple, compound, and complex sentences to achieve this effect. You can change your sentence structure to draw attention to particular topics. For example, a shorter sentence can draw attention to an important idea.

Where you place something in a sentence also indicates its importance in the overall message that you're trying to convey. If you want people to remember essential information, place it at the end of a sentence. People tend to forget the middle of sentences, so you can place the least important information in the middle of your sentence.

- Since Lucy has been studying hard, her grades have improved, and she could qualify for a grant. (Most important idea mentioned last,)
- Lucy has been studying hard, and her grades have improved. She could qualify for a grant. (Most important point in its own short sentence.)

Active and Passive Voice

Active voice and passive voice are two ways to determine who is doing the action in a sentence. While the style for business and especially academic documents used to be passive, formal, and wordy, these days documents need to be mostly in active voice, which makes them clearer and easier to understand.

To write well-structured sentences in active voice, you have to understand the differences between active voice and passive voice.

Let's start by looking at a simple sentence in active voice.

- I buy a sandwich.

This sentence is straightforward, and it's clear that the subject, I, does something to the object, a sandwich.

If you turn this sentence around, so that the object takes the place of the subject: "A sandwich is bought by me" you're looking at the passive voice. This means your sentences become longer and somewhat awkward.

Passive voice can sometimes be a good option, for example, if you don't want to appear to blame someone for a negative action, "The window was broken." You don't know who broke the window.

Here's a trick that helps identify passive voice. First, look through your document and notice where the forms of the verb "to be" appear. These forms include "is, are, was, were, be, being, been." ("Am" is another form of the verb "to be," but it really doesn't appear in passive voice.) Once you have found a "to be" verb, try adding "by zombies" to the end of the sentence. If those words fit and make a sensible sentence, you have passive voice.

- Carl broke the window. No "to be" verb; can't add "by zombies"—active voice
- The window was broken. The window was ("to be" verb) broken (could add "by zombies")—passive voice
- Maria is the CEO. Maria is ("to be" verb) the CEO (can't add "by zombies")—active voice

Key Takeaways

- Good grammar will make it easier to get your message across.
- Word order and sentence structure create meaning.
- Plain English has a straightforward sentence structure which will help your audience understand your message better.
- There are four types of basic sentence structures in English—simple sentences, compound sentences, complex sentences, and compound-complex sentences. Plain English does not usually use compound-complex sentences, as they can be harder to follow.
- Don't combine too many ideas into one sentence.

- Make sure you vary your sentence structure, as it's difficult to read a series of short, choppy sentences or long, complicated ones.

In Chapter 4, we're going to look at capitalization and punctuation.

CHAPTER 4

Capitalization and Punctuation

Capitalization and punctuation are important parts of plain English writing. Capitalization adds emphasis to certain words, and punctuation affects how a sentence reads. They help readers find their way through a sentence. Capitalization tells what words are important. Punctuation separates different parts of sentences, ends sentences, provides "signposts" about what type of text is coming next, and more.

Many people consider capitalization and punctuation—especially punctuation—to be difficult subjects. There are a number of rules, but you will probably not use all of them in one piece of writing. In fact, in writing one paragraph, you are likely to use only a few capital letters and a few marks of punctuation.

Here's a look at the most important uses for capital letters and punctuation marks.

Capitalization

There are two kinds of letters used when writing in plain English: capital letters and lowercase letters. Capital letters are also called uppercase letters or "caps."

- THESE ARE CAPITAL LETTERS
- these are lowercase letters

As you can see from any of the sentences in this book, most of the letters that make up English sentences are lowercase. Lowercase letters are used for most of the words in a sentence.

Capital letters are used for specific reasons. Most of these may be familiar to you, but there are some special cases that may not be.

Initial Capitals

You capitalize a letter when it is the first, or initial, letter of the first word in a sentence. Even the words "a," "an," and "the" are capitalized at the beginning of a sentence.

- You have received the memo.
- Everyone must clock in at the beginning of their shift.
- The policy applies to everyone.
- A delivery will arrive on Wednesday.

You also capitalize a letter when it is the first letter of a person's name. The first letter of the middle name and last name are capitalized too.

- Bob Cunningham
- Anton Lee Brown
- Leslie Snyder-Rose.

Another way that capital letters are used is as the first letter of a "proper noun," such as the name of a city, state, or country.

- Chicago
- Ohio
- France

Each part of a name that has more than one word is capitalized

- Los Angeles
- West Virginia

- South Africa

Use a lower-case letter for a general word, but a capital letter for a specific one.
- Go to the local library.
- Go to the Montgomery County Library.

Title Case

Usually, only the first word in a sentence is capitalized. However, when you have a title, heading, section, or subsection of a document, more than one word is capitalized. This is called "title case." You can see examples of title case used for subheadings throughout this book.

All of the words in a title or heading are capitalized except for a few. You don't capitalize the words "the," "a," or "an" unless they are the first word in the title. You also don't capitalize prepositions of two or three letters. Prepositions of four or more letters can be capitalized. Here are some examples.
- A Guide to Capitalization

In this example, "A" is the first word, so it is capitalized. "Guide" and "Capitalization" are nouns in the title, so they are capitalized too. The word "to" is a preposition of two letters, so it remains lowercase.
- Our Trip Through Egypt

In this example, all of the words are capitalized because "through" is a preposition of seven letters. If the heading is "Our Trip to Egypt," "to" would not be capitalized because it has fewer than four letters.

It's possible to write a sentence in all capital letters, but it's not advisable. It does make a point more forcefully, but it comes across like shouting. All caps are considered rude, particularly in online social media. You could use all caps in an advertisement or sales brochure to make an important point or draw the customer's eye to a special feature, offer, or piece of information.

Acronyms

You see acronyms all the time in business writing. Acronyms are like abbreviations that are made up of the first letters of the separate words in a business name, an organization, or a familiar expression. There is no punctuation between the letters of the acronym, and short words like "to" and "the" are often not included in the acronym.

- NASA—National Aeronautics and Space Administration
- WHO—World Health Organization
- ASAP—As Soon As Possible
- CEO—Chief Executive Officer

Many of these acronyms are general knowledge and don't need spelling out. However, if you have an acronym that is not familiar to your readers, you should spell out the words the first time you use it and put the whole version in parentheses. After that, you can just use the acronym.

- You should contact the National Labor Relations Board (NLRB). The NLRB will help you with your problem.

Punctuation

There are some basic punctuation marks that you should know. The period (.), question mark (?), exclamation mark (!), comma (,), quotation marks (""), parentheses () and dashes (—), and apostrophe ('), are the main ones. There are also a hyphen (-), colon (:), and semicolon (;). They are not used as often, but we'll discuss them anyway, just in case you need them.

There are a lot of different punctuation marks, so we'll start with the most important ones. The "end punctuation" marks are the period, question mark, and exclamation mark.

Period

Most sentences end with a period. That's why it's also called a "full stop."

- Our new vice-president is starting on Tuesday.
- The company picnic was a big success.

Periods also come after abbreviations. An abbreviation is a way to shorten a word or phrase by leaving out some of the letters. Abbreviations of titles—Mr., Mrs., Ms.—are the most often used. Another common abbreviation is etc., which means "and so on."

- Mr. Martinez is Ms. Smith's new assistant.
- For the display booth, we will need fliers, signs, pens, a banner, etc.

Question Marks and Exclamation Points

Question marks and exclamation points also end sentences. As their names imply, they are used when asking a question or making an exclamation.

- What are you doing next week?
- How do I fill out this form?
- This month's sales were the highest all year!
- Everyone in the sales department had an outstanding year!

Comma

Commas are very common marks of punctuation because they have a lot of uses. One way they are used is to set off items in a series or list.

- You will find scissors, tape, and a thumb drive in the top drawer.
- Name badges, tote bags, and note pads will be supplied to all attendees.

Commas are also used between independent clauses, before the conjunction (remember FANBOYS from Chapter 3).

- Someone will be in charge of the refreshments, but someone else will be in charge of the games.
- James has to work this week, and Roberto has to work next week.

There is a comma between a dependent clause and an independent clause if the dependent clause comes first, but not if the independent clause comes first.

- Because she is working by herself, Beth will not have the report done tomorrow.
- Beth will not have the report done tomorrow because she is working by herself.

Quotation Marks

Quotation marks go around reported speech—something that someone says.

- Marco said, "I will volunteer to work this weekend."
- "I will volunteer to work this weekend," Marco said.

As you can see, periods and commas go inside the quotation marks, every time, whether it involves reported speech or not.

Quotation marks can also go around a word that is being defined.

- The cargo will be hauled in "reefers," or refrigerated trucks.
- A "coin purse" holds small change.
- "Profiteroles" is another name for cream puffs.

Apostrophe

An apostrophe is used in contractions to take the place of missing letters.

- there is—there's
- you will—you'll
- are not—aren't

The most important use for apostrophes is to show possession. There are a few rules that apply to apostrophes and possession. Here are the most common.

If something belongs to a single person or thing, you add -'s to the name or word.

- John's car was damaged in the crash.
- The dog's leash is by the door.
- The manager's desk is bigger than mine.

If something belongs to a plural noun, you put an apostrophe after the -s.

- The cheerleaders' outfits are red and yellow.
- Our packages' labels are computer-generated.
- If you want the employees' email addresses, you'll have to ask them.

Parentheses and Dashes

Parentheses are used to enclose something that is not essential to a sentence. The words in parentheses can add information to a sentence that isn't necessary to understand the sentence but that clarifies the meaning of a word or words.

- Rafael can go to East Fifth Street (our second location) this weekend.
- I want to know what Stephen is doing (and not doing).
- My computer (the one in my study) just crashed.

Another way to set off something that is not absolutely necessary in a sentence is to use a dash or dashes. Most of the time, parentheses are good enough, but if you want to add extra emphasis, use dashes.

- The third order this week—the one that went to Idaho—was the biggest one.
- I want to have two waitresses—the best ones—scheduled on Saturdays.

Hyphen

A hyphenated word is one that has two parts that have to be connected in order to understand the meaning. For example, vice-president is hyphenated because the reader needs to understand that it's a certain kind of president—someone who assists the president. You can't do without the hyphen because "vice" is a word on its own with a different meaning. You can use the word "vice" with a hyphen and other words: vice-principal, for example.

Hyphens are also used to create a certain kind of adjective, a compound adjective that comes before a noun.

- a fast-acting drug. The drug isn't a fast drug. It isn't an acting drug. It's a fast-acting drug, meaning that it works quickly.
- the sixth-grade student. It isn't the sixth student. It isn't a grade student. It's a sixth-grade student.
- a Spanish-speaking interpreter. It isn't an interpreter who is Spanish. It's an interpreter who speaks Spanish.

You can also use a hyphen to separate a prefix and a word that uses the same letter: re-elect instead of reelect, for instance.

Colon

A colon is used to introduce something. It can be a single word.

- There is one thing you need to do this job well: confidence.

More often, what follows a colon is a list.
- Gather the ingredients you need for making the cookies: sugar, flour, milk, and eggs.
- There are two essential parts to any sentence: the subject and the verb.

If what follows the colon is a complete sentence, it begins with a capital letter.
- The boss had one requirement: Every employee must come to work on time.

Semicolon

The semicolon can be used to join two independent clauses. Each of the two parts could be a separate sentence. The two independent clauses should be closely related in meaning.
- Julia and Ken get to work at the same time; they leave at the same time, too.

If you don't use the semicolon, you have just made a run-on sentence. A run-on sentence is one that puts two independent clauses together with no punctuation or with just a comma. Run-on sentences are an example of bad grammar.
- Julia and Ken get to work at the same time they leave at the same time too.
- Julia and Ken get to work at the same time, they leave at the same time too.

Key Takeaways

- Capitalization and punctuation are important to help convey meaning in your writing. They tell what's important and how to read sentences.
- Capital letters are used at the beginning of a sentence, for names and proper nouns, and for most of the words in a title or heading.
- Punctuation marks include the period, question mark, exclamation point, comma, quotation marks, parentheses, dashes, apostrophe, hyphen, colon, and semicolon.
- Punctuation is used at the ends of sentences and to separate clauses. Periods and commas are the marks of punctuation that you will use most often.

In the next chapter, we'll take a look at how to plan for better plain English writing.

CHAPTER 5

Planning Your Writing

Writing starts long before your fingers hit the keyboard. Writing doesn't just come automatically to anyone. You have to use your brain. You have to plan.

No doubt you've heard the saying, "Proper Prior Planning Prevents Poor Performance." You may even have a sign like that in your workplace. It's true for many aspects of business, and it's certainly true of writing in plain English. Planning before you begin writing a document will help ensure that the result is readable, understandable, and effective.

Consider Your Readers

You need to think carefully about who the audience is for your topic. If you know your audience, it will be easier to decide what type of information to include in your text and also what layout will contribute to your readers' understanding.

The most successful documents discuss topics from the perspective of the reader and not the writer. It can help to develop a profile of your readers before you start writing.

Who Is Your Target Audience?

Who is going to be reading your writing—whom should you be writing for? Are you writing an email for your salesforce? Or should it be addressed to all your employees? Are you writing a letter to a vendor or supplier? Are you writing an ad designed to get new customers or one to introduce a new product to existing customers? Will you be issuing a new employee handbook or communicating a new procedure? Do you need to create a list of instructions or explain a process? Answers to these questions will help you formulate your writing plan.

One important thing to know about your readers is how well they know the subject you're going to be communicating about. If they're knowledgeable about the topic, you may have an easier time writing something that they will easily understand. You can use terms that are specific to your area of business without having to explain them. If they're not already familiar with your topic, you may have to explain some of the basics as you write.

If you're not sure about what basic knowledge your readers have, it's best to assume they're intelligent but not necessarily familiar with your topic. Your writing may have to explain certain concepts. At the same time, though, you don't want to talk down to them. That's where plain English can help you. The principles of writing in plain English that you have been learning will serve you well.

You should also consider your readers' needs and expectations. If you're writing a sales brochure, it should be upbeat and conversational. If you're explaining a new company policy to employees, you will want to be more serious and straightforward. Writing a series of instructions for completing a process will need to be clear and presented in a specific order.

What Do Your Readers Need to Know?

Planning your writing involves figuring out what your readers need to know and then giving it to them. Think about your topic—the major points that you want to make—and what subtopics contribute to it. The major points can become your paragraphs, and the subtopics can be either sentences that make up the paragraphs or other sections of your document.

Your main ideas should be clear to you before you begin working on your document. Make a list of things that need to be part of it. You can organize your ideas by grouping similar or related ones together.

For example, if your main idea for the document is ways to improve sales, you might want to have paragraphs on training, advertising, and incentives. Then take the first one—training—and list some things you want to say about that. You might want to talk about teaming new employees with existing mentors. Another sentence or subtopic might recommend books or videos on sales. Then move on to listing some ideas under the topic of advertising. Pretty soon, you'll have the skeleton of a document that just needs to be fleshed out.

On the other hand, you might want to create separate documents for each subtopic: training, advertising, and incentives. Sometimes it's better to have only one major idea per document. If you have a document with several major sections, it becomes more difficult to read.

The Importance of Layout

The words you put in your document are important, but how the document looks is important too. The layout and graphics can make a piece of writing more attractive and more readable as well. Of course, if you're sending a simple email, you may not have much layout to consider—but there are still some basic principles that will help even then.

Keeping it simple is the first rule of good layout. You don't want to add elements that you don't need to get your message across. You may think that cute pieces of clip art will jazz up your memo, but they'll really just distract from your message. If an illustration is necessary, by all means include it, but don't add graphics just for the sake of adding them. For example, a diagram of the proper way to lift a box would be important for safety information, but a drawing of a fall leaf adds nothing to a document, even if it comes out in September.

Important design elements will depend on the nature of the document. Most official communications should include your company's logo. You can use your letterhead for external communications, but it may not be necessary for internal memos.

What are some important design elements? White space, headings and subheadings, color, and images are all things to be considered.

White Space

You might not think that the blank space between blocks of text are as important as the text itself. While white space doesn't actually convey any information, it can make the document easier to read and understand. Readers find solid blocks of text intimidating. Some space between them relieves the eyes and gives them a place to rest. That's why you have separate paragraphs—not just to contain separate ideas, but to break up the text into manageable bits.

Headings and Subheadings

Adding headings and subheadings fulfills several functions. Of course, they help the reader understand the organization of a document. But in addition to providing a map through the document, they give the document a break so that it isn't a single block of gray-looking text.

If you divide your document into headings and subheadings, you will want to make sure the reader can tell which is which. Make your major headings a larger size than the subheadings, for example. You can see examples of the different sizes of headings and subheadings throughout this book.

Structure

Your document needs to be set out in a logical way. Headings and subheadings emphasize the structure of your writing, which determines how the audience will read the text. Think of headings as signposts that guide your readers through a document and let them know what is coming next.

Organizing your document, especially longer documents like reports, should be part of your planning process. Documents can be organized alphabetically, chronologically, or according to the themes or processes followed. Choose a structure that is best suited to your type of document. Alphabetical organization, for example, is useful for a glossary or index. Chronological structure can be used to show a company's history.

Probably the most common structure is by theme. That's where headings and subheadings really come in handy. Headings often summarize the sections that follow them.

You can double-check the structure of your document by printing it so that you can see the flow of your headings. You can also use the outline view in your word processing program to help with this.

Color

While you probably don't need to add color to add color to emails or new pages for the employee handbook, you may want color in your ads, brochures, PowerPoint presentations, or other documents. Color adds interest and can aid readability.

Of course, color can actually harm readability if it's not used correctly. One thing you need to consider is contrast. Text is more readable if the background color is one that contrasts with the lettering. For example, orange type will be difficult to read on a background of red, no matter how bright it is. The two colors simply don't contrast with each other. Advertisers know that the color combinations with the most contrast are yellow and red or yellow and black, which is why you see so many ads, logos, and signs featuring those colors.

"Reversed-out" type is when the type is white on a black or other dark background. The important word here is "dark." Reversed-out type is nearly impossible to read against light colors like yellow or sky blue. It's very hard on the eyes.

Type also does not read well on top of an image, no matter what color it is.

Images

Images can really illustrate and support your text, but they can also overshadow it. Achieving a balance between the two is important. Too many images in too little space can make the document feel crowded and difficult to read.

If you don't have a design department to supply them, the kinds of images that you can put in a document include:

- illustrations
- clip art
- stock photos

(Even if you do have a design department, you should keep an eye on them to make sure they don't get carried away with reversed-out type or text on top of images.)

A picture may not really be worth a thousand words, but the combination of images and words is particularly powerful. One way to combine text and images successfully is the "infographic." As the name suggests, infographics convey information in a graphic form. Some types of infographics are:

- line graphs
- bar graphs
- pie charts
- maps
- illustrations
- flow charts
- timelines
- bulleted lists

Infographics

Infographics present information in an easily understandable way without requiring long explanations. People remember information better if it's presented in visual form. Infographics are especially useful when you have to convey complex processes or interpret statistics.

Infographics are useful for documents such as how-to guides, comparisons of benefits, and even recipe books. They're a great way to explain new concepts to children in school textbooks, but they're also helpful for adults who need to interpret information.

If you do decide to use infographics, make sure that they are appropriate to your text and they are understandable rather than more confusing. The best infographics use graphics and text to provide information in an engaging and entertaining way that is also easy to understand, especially for people who don't necessarily speak English as a first language.

There are several uses for infographics:

- The *informational* infographic is the best option if you want to provide people with new information and educate them about a topic.
- Use the *statistical* infographic when you want to display data sets visually. You can use visuals like pie charts to convey your information.
- A *process* infographic can display a step-by-step process visually, usually in a graphic information flow from left to right or top to bottom.
- A *comparison* infographic can be helpful when it comes to comparing two options. The data or pieces of information are usually presented in a two-column layout.

While infographic designs are different based on their function, they usually have the same basic structure.

- The headline tells you what is happening in the infographic. It should be short so that it can make an impact.
- The caption should summarize the information in the infographic or give the reader an explanation of how to read it.
- The body is the most important part, where you present your main ideas. Make sure you use visuals like charts, tables, and icons.
- The conclusion summarizes the information discussed and can also include a "call to action," a text prompt

that inspires your readers to do something—buy a product, do further research on the topic, or share the information, for example.

- You should include your sources so readers can verify the information if they need or want to. For instance, if you have an infographic about the calorie count of various foods, you might note that it came from the FDA or USDA.

The basic principles of document design apply to infographics as well.

- Don't use too many fonts, as the document can quickly become confusing. Use about three at the most. The header font can be slightly decorative, but the rest of the font must be plain and easy to read.
- When it comes to layout, it's also important to make sure the pages of your document have enough white space and that they're not stuffed full of text and images.
- The colors of your infographic should match the tone of the text and the information that you're trying to convey. For example, use dark or muted colors for a serious topic. If it's a fun topic, you can play around with color.
- Make sure that the text in an infographic is large enough to be easily legible. Your reader shouldn't have to work too hard to get the information. Infographics are supposed to make reading easier.

Before using your infographic to share information, ask your coworkers or friends if they understand what the infographic is saying. You want to make sure that the visuals and text are working together to convey a clear message. See below an example of an infographic, which is both informational and shows a process.

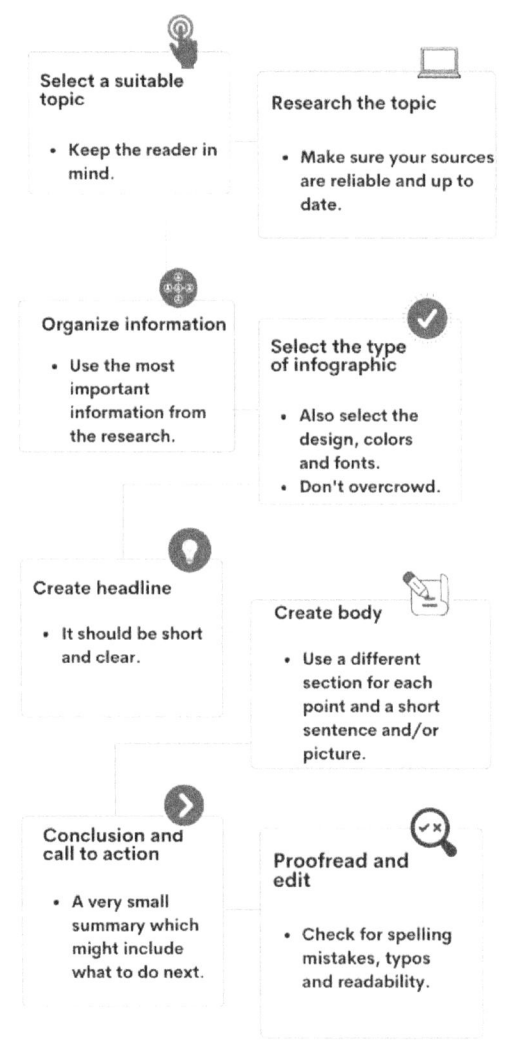

(Foster, 2022)

Planning the Look of Your Text

Once you've written your text, you should give some attention to the way you present it. When compiling a document that's easily readable, it's important to also consider the format and layout. There's nothing worse than having a document written in words that is easy to understand, but the font is too small to read or the background is cluttered with designs that make it difficult to see what is going on.

Luckily, once you know what to do, layout is one of the easier aspects of your document to sort out. If you don't have the time to do it yourself, you can hire a graphic designer to do it for you. But you still need to know a little something about layout to instruct them on what you want and to supervise their work.

The type you use for your text is the most important part of a document. You can establish a style that you use for all your documents, or you can use different styles depending on your purpose. You can set these styles up before you begin writing, or you can apply them to your document once it's complete.

Type

You may not notice it, but all texts are made up of type, and there are different kinds of type. There are a number of choices you can make when it comes to what your text looks like: fonts, type size, type style, line spacing, and alignment. You can make changes to all of these aspects of type in your word processing or graphics program.

Typefaces

When it comes to "fonts," or typefaces, you want your audience to be able to read without difficulty. Word processing programs like Microsoft Word and Google Docs have a wide range of fonts available, and it's not always easy to know what to choose. Fonts are divided into the "serif" and "sans serif" types. A serif font has a small projection at the end of the stroke in most letters. Sans serif fonts don't have this. Examples of serif fonts are Times New Roman and Georgia (the font this book is written in). Sans serif fonts include Helvetica and Arial, two of the most popular typefaces in the world.

When you choose a font, consider if your text will be printed or read online. Serif fonts like Times New Roman are often chosen for long, printed reports and other serious communications. Sans serif fonts are often used for websites, ads, and text headings. Don't use too many different fonts in one document, as this will only confuse your readers.

Type Size

Type comes in different sizes, from small to large, measured in "points." The smallest type sizes are very difficult to read and will frustrate your audience. Larger type is easier to read—but text that is too large makes a bad impression and doesn't really make a document easier to read.

What size type should you use? A good standard is 12-point or 14-point type for body text, especially in emails. Titles, headings, and subheads can be a bit larger. "Display" headlines for ads are often in much larger type—20- or 24-point.

Type Style

There are several different "styles" of type you can use. Think of the body text of your document as the basic style and the other ones as variations used to add emphasis.

Bold-faced type adds the most emphasis. It is most often used for headings, but it can also be used for important information such as safety warnings: The slicing machine is dangerous when it is turned on. **Do not place your hands or fingers near the blade.**

Italic type adds less emphasis than bold type. It's often used to stress a word in a text that you want to define for readers. For example: Use an *infographic*, or visual information, to convey statistics.

<u>Underlined</u> type can be used for whole sentences you want to emphasize: <u>You will not be allowed back in the building after closing time.</u>

Spacing

Line spacing is the amount of white space that appears between lines of type and between paragraphs. How you use line spacing can affect the readability of your document.

Single-spacing your text can make it harder to read. The lines appear crowded together, which places extra pressure on your eyes when it comes to following the lines. You'll find 1.15 and 1.5 spacing are the standards for text that is the most suitable and the easiest to read. Double spacing leads to large white spaces between the lines of text and can cause readers to miss information.

Alignment

The alignment of text on the page is called "justification." It will most likely show up in your word processor controls under "align and indent." Left-aligned text means that the left side of the text appears in a straight line down the side. This is the easiest to read. It's also called "right ragged" because the right edge of the text doesn't line up vertically the way the left side does.

Justified text means that the text goes in a straight vertical line down both sides of the text. This book is written with justified text. It looks good in many instances and is often used for longer, more formal pieces of writing like reports. However, it can be difficult to read, as there can be big spaces between words and sentences.

Right-aligned text is almost never used, except once in a while in advertising.

Key Takeaways

- Before you write anything, you need to plan. You can start your process of writing plain English texts by considering the purpose of your document.
- Know the audience for your document. Think about their needs and expectations. Successful communication discusses topics from the readers' perspective. To help you, develop a profile of your typical reader before you start writing.
- Use headings and subheadings to lead your reader through your writing. Attention to structure will pay off in effective communication.
- Think about the design elements of your document such as layout, text, images, and styles. What will best help get your point across?
- You can present information visually by using infographics. These can include pie charts and other illustrations. People often find it easier to remember information if the document contains infographics.

Plan the structure of an infographic. Make sure that the visuals and text work together to convey your message.

- Consider readability when you select your font and text alignment. A font of size 12 points should be large enough for your audience to read.
- Don't use too many different kinds of font. Your audience will be distracted by them and become confused.
- Text is usually easier to read when it's left-aligned.

In chapter 6, we will discuss three kinds of language to avoid in plain English writing—jargon, idioms, and nominalization.

CHAPTER 6

What to Avoid in Plain English Writing

We've covered a lot of things you should do in order to write clear, understandable text. Now let's take a look at some of the things *not* to do. Jargon, idioms, and nominalization make writing difficult and confusing to any audience, but they're even more of a problem when you're addressing someone who isn't a native speaker of English.

Using jargon means hiding meaning behind terms and abbreviations that the general public doesn't understand. Idioms are a way of using words that don't say what they really mean. There are various kinds of nominalization; all of them make other parts of speech into nouns, which is confusing.

Fortunately, you can replace these forms of language with clear, understandable, plain English. We'll show you how.

Jargon

Jargon consists of words that are specific to a certain group or profession. People outside those groups have a hard time knowing what the writer is talking about because they just aren't familiar with the words. Unfortunately, you run into jargon-filled writing every day. It's like being talked down to. Jargon emphasizes that there are insiders and outsiders, and puts up a barrier between people based on what words they recognize.

There are lots of fields that have their own jargon, but some of the most common are computer-related terms, business language, legal writing, and medical information. Here's a look at the words that insiders use and what they really mean in plain English.

Computer

It's easy to feel confusted when it comes to computer jargon. It sounds high-tech, trendy, and intelligent, but if you don't know what it means, you feel inadequate and lost. A piece of text filled with computer jargon might look like this:

The beta version of the new server software has insufficient bandwidth to accommodate the range of cloud computing that would be required for this application. Multiple bugs have been found in the code.

Here are some common examples of computer jargon and their plain English translations.

- A *beta version* is a test version of a piece of software or hardware. It usually goes to *beta testers,* who try out the product and make note of problems.
- *Lines of code* are the instructions in a program that tell the computer what to do. Programmers produce lines of code when they're writing software.
- A *bug* is a flaw in a product, especially in software. If a piece of software is *buggy,* it doesn't work like it's supposed to.
- *Hard copy* is a printed version of a document. Hard copy is also called a *print-out.*
- *RAM* and *ROM* stand for Random Access Memory and Read-Only Memory. RAM stores your files while you are working on them. ROM is a permanent memory that stores instructions for your computer. Memory is measured in *gigabytes* (gigs) and *terabytes.*

- *Backup* is both a noun and a verb. A backup is a copy you make of something that you're working on so that you can restore your work if your computer crashes. To back up means to make that copy. You can have a backup drive that stores the whole contents of your computer.
- *Bandwidth* means how quickly a computer can transmit data. Faster bandwidths can send more data in a shorter time. (Some businesses also use "bandwidth" as slang to mean how much work a certain number of employees can do within a given time.)
- The *cloud* is a way to have computer work done or stored outside of your own network. It uses "remote servers" to perform work.
- *Cookies* are small lines of text that are stored on a computer so that a website will recognize a customer when they return. They are stored in a *cache* on your computer, which you can empty to make more room.

It's a good idea to replace computer jargon with plain English. For example, if you are discussing a personal music player, instead of saying that it has 128 gigabytes of storage, say that it will hold 5,000 songs.

Business

You would think that business language ought to be straightforward. Businesses sell products and/or services. However, internally, businesses use jargon-filled language that a new employee, for example, might not understand. What would you make of a text like this?

This recent hire seems weak in her core competencies and neglects opportunities that are low-hanging fruit. She appears to add nothing to our synergies. Nonetheless, we should circle back and see if training can empower her. Keep me in the loop.

- *Due diligence* is something that businesses do when they're looking at another company for merger or acquisition. They investigate the financial health of the other company's finances. It means taking appropriate care before investing money in a business venture.
- *Laser-focused* just means really focused. Lasers have nothing to do with it. It sounds more impressive but really means nothing. Saying a company is "laser-focused on improved sales" doesn't actually say anything.
- *Impressions* are the number of people who see an ad. For example, "If we advertise in this magazine, we will receive 10,000 impressions per month."
- *Attrition* means that something, usually the number of employees, is going down naturally. A company that cuts its staff by attrition, for instance, is waiting for employees to leave rather than firing them.
- *Benchmarks* are measures of how well something is doing. You can have benchmarks for sales or production, for instance, and that means you have targets or goals in place.
- *Best practices* are strategies that have been tested and proven. They have evidence to back them up.
- To *punt* (actually a football term) means to stop doing something that isn't successful—for example, to stop spending money on advertising when it isn't getting responses.

- To *empower* someone is to give them the authority to decide something or the ability to do something.
- *Bleeding edge* is a term that means "at the forefront" of something, such as technology. "Cutting edge" used to mean the same thing, but "bleeding edge" sounds even more modern.
- *Core competency* simply means someone's main skill or area of expertise.
- *Low-hanging fruit* means something that is easy to accomplish and can be done first. "Low-hanging fruit" in sales would be customers that are already willing to buy the product.
- *In the loop* means being informed of a piece of news.
- *Synergy* (or sometimes *synergies*) is a word that is used to describe what happens when two or more people work together on something. Sometimes it is also used to describe benefits that arise when two companies merge.
- *Circle back* means to revisit a topic later or to plan a follow-up meeting.
- *Deliverables* are simply products—things that are delivered to customers.

Legal Jargon

Legal jargon is used a lot. Contracts in particular are virtually unreadable, which leads people to sign them without understanding them. Things are looking up, though—"The language used in law is changing. Many lawyers are now adopting a plain English style. Even so, there are still legal phrases that baffle non-lawyers (*A to Z of legal phrases.* (n.d.)).

Here's a look at some of them.

- An *addendum* or *amendment* is language that adds something to or changes something in an existing contract.
- *Arbitration* or *mediation* is a way to solve a disagreement without going to court. A person or group is assigned to talk to the two sides to see what kind of solution will be agreeable to both of them.
- *Breach of contract* is when someone doesn't do what they promised to in an agreement or contract.
- *Damages* means money owed to someone because of a lawsuit about an accident, for example, or a breach of contract.
- *Civil procedure* is a court case about contracts, lawsuits, or trials other than criminal trials.
- *Insolvency* and *indigent* mean having no money. *Indigent* can also be a noun that means a person who has no money.
- *Litigation* is a trial or lawsuit—something that has to go to court.
- *Annulment* means saying that something isn't valid, like a marriage or a contract. Reasons for an annulment include fraud or, in the case of a marriage, being forced into it.
- *Appellant* is someone who files an appeal, such as trying to overturn a conviction.
- *Bench* just means the judge in a trial.
- *Decree* is a decision issued by a judge.
- *Statutes* are laws.

- A *consideration* is something, usually money, that is given in exchange for a sale or a service, for example.
- *Default* means that someone has not answered a lawsuit or not lived up to an agreement, and the decision automatically goes against them.
- An *injunction* is a legal decision that someone is not allowed to do something. A restraining order is one form of an injunction.
- A *signatory* is simply someone who signs a contract. Sometimes in a contract, you will see the words "hereinafter known as the party of the first part (or second part)." This refers to the person proposing the contract and the person agreeing to the contract.

Medical Jargon

People in the medical field use language that's not easy to understand. Diagnoses and instructions are littered with acronyms and technical terms that seem to hide what is actually being said. Even over-the-counter medicine documentation uses long, technical words that are difficult, especially for people whose first language isn't English. Here's an example.

This adult nasal spray is for local application in the nose to give symptomatic relief of nasal congestion (including in colds), perennial and allergic rhinitis (including hayfever) and sinusitis.

What does this mean in plain English? Let's look at a better way to state this information.

Use this spray for adults only. It will help relieve stuffed-up nose, inflamed sinuses, and hay fever. Spray directly into the nose (Medical information. (n.d.)).

These are some more technical terms or pieces of medical jargon.

- An *analgesic* is a pain reliever—either aspirin or something stronger.
- *Antipyretic* means a medicine that fights fever.
- *Idiopathic* means "of unknown origin." For example, knee pain would be called idiopathic if the doctor doesn't know what is causing it.
- *AMA* has two meanings. First, it means Against Medical Advice. An example of this might be someone who leaves the emergency room before the doctors are finished stitching their wounds. AMA also stands for American Medical Association, a national organization of medical professionals.
- *Dialysis* is a way of filtering the blood to remove toxins. You most often hear the word in the context of kidney dialysis.
- *H and P* stands for History and Physical, the first thing a doctor does when they see a new patient. History involves asking questions about when the illness started, family history of disease, etc. The physical examination includes taking blood pressure, listening to the patient's lungs, and so forth.
- *Discharge* has two meanings. It can mean releasing a person from a hospital. It can also mean a substance that comes out of a wound or body part. Pus is an example of a discharge.
- *Enuresis* means bedwetting.
- *Hepatic/renal/cardiac/pedal.* These terms refer to different body parts. Hepatic means the liver is

involved. Renal is for the kidneys, and cardiac is for the heart. Pedal refers to the foot.

- *Cyanotic* means that a person appears to be blue due to lack of oxygen.
- *Hemorrhage* is extreme, rapid bleeding.
- *Jaundice* is yellowing of the skin or eyes.
- *LOL in NAD* means "little old lady in no apparent distress." It's a way of referring to an older woman who appears to have nothing wrong with her. It's a kind of code phrase among doctors in an emergency room, for example.
- A *neoplasm* is a tumor.
- *ECG (or EKG)* and *EEG* are acronyms meaning electrocardiogram, a test for the heart; and electroencephalogram, a test for the brain.
- *Palliative care* means treating the symptoms without curing the underlying disease. One example would be treating a patient for pain when they are nearing death from cancer.
- To *triage* is to assess patients based on how severe their injuries are. Emergency room personnel often have to triage patients to determine who should be treated first.
- *Sepsis* is a severe infection that affects the whole body.

Idioms

Idioms are phrases that don't use words literally. They are similar to cliches and can be very difficult for non-native English speakers to understand. You can easily replace them with plain English terms instead.

- *Bang for your buck* means getting a big return or a good deal on what you spend. It's often used in advertising. "Return on investment" is another way of saying this.
- *Chiseled in stone* means an instruction or other procedure that you must perform without any change. "That policy is not chiseled in stone" means that there may be exceptions to the policy.
- *Under the weather* has nothing to do with weather. It means that someone is a little bit ill or not feeling well.
- *Take it with a grain of salt* means to be skeptical of something. You might say, "Don't believe everything you hear" instead.
- To *go down in flames* means to fail spectacularly.
- To *see eye to eye* means to agree.
- *Beat around the bush* means to avoid making a direct statement. "Why don't you just come out and say it?" is an appropriate response.
- *Bend over backward* means to go to great lengths. For example, you might say that a salesperson bends over backward to close a deal.
- *Bite off more than you can chew* means to take on a project that is too large for one person to do.
- *The ball is in your court* means a decision is yours to make. "It's up to you" is a good alternative.
- *Crunch time* is when you are rapidly approaching a deadline and must work extra hard.
- A *skeleton crew* is one that has only the bare minimum of necessary workers.

- To *go the extra mile* is to do more than what needs to be done.
- A *no-brainer* is a decision that is easy to make.

Nominalization

Nominalization means making a noun out of another part of speech such as a verb or adjective. It makes words unnecessarily long and difficult, which makes whole sentences more difficult to read. Here are some examples of nominalization.

Gerunds

Gerunds are verb forms that end in -ing and take the place of nouns. For example, in the sentence, "He hates being here," *being* is the gerund, from the verb "to be." You can tell this because you would be able to replace the gerund with "it."— "He hates it." In the sentence, "Swimming is good exercise," *swimming* is the gerund, from the verb "to swim." You could replace the gerund with the word "it"— "It is good exercise."

Noun Phrases

If you said, "Swimming 20 laps is good exercise," the whole phrase "swimming 20 laps" is a noun phrase. This might cause difficulty reading, because at first you might think that the verb form should be "are" because the plural word "laps" is right next to the verb. But since the whole phrase is equivalent to a single noun, the verb has to be "is." It can be quite confusing.

Another example is "Where you go next is up to you." The phrase "where you go next" is a noun phrase. All four words together take the place of a noun, which is the subject of the sentence. Again, you could replace the words with "it"—"It is up to you."

Endings

Verbs and adjectives can be made into nouns by adding any of a number of endings, or *suffixes*, to them. This form of nominalization is sometimes called "nouning." For example, "The game was canceled on account of rain" would become "The game suffered cancellation on account of rain." This sentence is longer, wordier, and more difficult to understand. It sounds more formal than it needs to be.

Here are some endings that can make a verb into a noun.

- -er or -or (the verb *teach* becomes *teacher*, a noun)
- -tion or -ation (*operate* becomes *operation*)
- -sion (*discuss* becomes *discussion*)
- -ment (*develop* becomes *development*)
- -ance or -ence (*accept* becomes *acceptance*)
- -ence or -ency (*depend* becomes *dependence* or *dependency*)
- -al (*refuse* becomes *refusal*)
- -y (*discover* becomes *discovery*)

Adjectives can also be made into nouns by adding endings.

- -ity (*stupid* becomes *stupidity*)
- -ty (*difficult* becomes *difficulty*)
- -ness (*thick* becomes *thickness*)
- -ility (*responsible* becomes *responsibility*)
- -cy (*accurate* becomes *accuracy*)

Nominalization is often followed by a preposition such as *of or about*, which makes the sentence even longer and harder to read. For example, "the difficulty of the situation" versus "the difficult situation" or versus "Our discussion about grammar was extensive" versus "We discussed grammar extensively."

Technical, scientific, and academic writing are full of nominalization, which is one reason that they are so difficult to read.

Key Takeaways

- Jargon, idioms, and nominalization make text difficult to read and understand.
- Jargon is technical terms from a specific field or profession.
- Idioms are phrases that aren't meant literally.
- Nominalization is making verbs or adjectives into nouns through the use of added endings or suffixes.
- Avoid using jargon, idioms, and nominalization to make your writing clearer. Use the verb or adjective form instead.

The next chapter will discuss how to review your writing before you publish, print, or send it.

CHAPTER 7

Review Your Writing

When you review your writing, you take the opportunity to step back and re-envision it. You think about the goals of your writing and whether you have accomplished these goals. You ensure that your ideas are clearly expressed and well-supported. And you make certain that errors of grammar and style do not detract from your work.

Reviewing and editing your work is the last chance you have to make a good first impression. Before you hit print or send, make sure that your writing is everything you want it to be.

Editing Your Work

The editing process is a step in writing a document that you shouldn't skip over. Think about how embarrassing it would be to send out an email and discover you've spelled the recipient's name wrong. Consider what a bad impression it would make if you have left out important information, such as how to contact you. A poorly written document can make the readers confused or even resentful. A text full of grammatical mistakes will be less likely to make people trust you with their business or lessons.

What are the steps to a good editing process?

Leave It Alone

Reviewing and editing can be an extensive process, but there are steps you can take to make it smooth and effective. After you write something, it's often best to leave it alone before you go back to it and start your reviewing process. You'll come back to it with fresh eyes. When you've first written something, you're not really able to see its flaws and mistakes. You read over the document too quickly and you're too close to it to review and edit effectively.

How long should you put your writing away for? That depends on the time you have available and the kind of writing you have created. If you've written something that has to go out that same day, try to leave it alone for at least a couple of hours—say, while you are on your lunch hour. If it's an email that really has to go out soon, see if you can wait till after your coffee break to review your document. If you've written a longer report or an advertising brochure, wait at least overnight until you try reading and editing it.

Read It Aloud

Reading your document aloud is a great way to spot mistakes. Why? Reading aloud makes you focus on every word rather than scanning or skimming over the text. You can read it to a friend or coworker, who may be able to hear when you have made a mistake that you yourself don't see. Don't forget that if you don't want to read out loud in the office, you can use the read aloud function on your software with some headphones. Many word processing programs have that feature.

If you notice a mistake while you're reading out loud, pause to correct it right away or at least mark on the document where the mistake is. You probably won't remember to make the correction if you don't make note of where and what the mistake is.

Use a Focus Group

If you have the time and the document is a longer, really important one, get some opinions from people who represent your expected readers. After they've read the text, ask them if they have any questions. This will reveal what parts of the document may be unclear. Ask them about key points in the document. For example, you can ask, "What does this say about the delivery times we're promising for our products?" or "Based on this document, when and how should you request vacation time?" The answers can be revealing—you may be surprised!

Take notes during the focus group or have someone else do it. Use the feedback you get to revise your writing. Look at the parts of your document that caused confusion and determine how you can improve them. If you have to do a lot of rewriting, it won't hurt to do another focus group with a different panel of readers to see how successful your revisions were. I always do this myself when I am writing assessments for students.

This may sound like a lot of work, but you'll find that it's time well spent. Your focus groups can help you avoid wasting time answering questions about points that weren't clear. You then won't lose business because customers don't understand your ads.

Software Tools

The word processing or other software that you used to create the document is almost certain to have built-in tools that can help you with editing and proofreading. Spelling checkers are essential, and grammar checkers can be helpful, too.

Just keep in mind that spelling and grammar checkers are not infallible. A spelling checker, for example, will see this as correct: "Did you get a letter form me?" The spelling checker will accept "form" as a real word and let it go. A grammar checker may "realize" that "from" is the word you really want.

But that's a mistake you could have caught if you read the document aloud.

Software tools like *Grammarly* and the *Hemingway Editor* can be worth the investment, especially if you're a sole entrepreneur and don't have a staff member who can check your work.

Professional Editing

Another option is to have a professional editor check your document. You may not have an editor on staff, but there are plenty of freelance editors who will gladly do the job. You can find them on sites like Indeed. It makes sense to hire a professional if your document is long and complicated, like an employee manual or a book.

Freelance editors and proofreaders charge by the hour or a flat fee for the whole project. As with any professional that you want to hire, you can ask for satisfied customers that you can contact.

It can also help if you ask the prospective editor whether they're familiar with the principles of plain English. That way they'll know not to combine shorter sentences into long, complicated sentences with multiple clauses.

The Editing Process

The editing process generally involves three stages: structural editing, copy editing, and proofreading. You look for different kinds of mistakes at each stage, so it's important not to skip one. Do them one at a time. That makes you reread the document multiple times with a different focus each time. You can catch different sorts of mistakes each time, until your document is "clean," or free from errors.

Structural Editing

Structural editing, as it says, means looking at the overall structure of your document. Ask yourself if you've included all the information your readers might need or if you need to remove anything. Have you set the document up with different paragraphs that follow logically? Does each paragraph need a heading or only certain ones? If you have more than one heading, you may want to consider making each one a separate document—three emails instead of one, for example.

Then look at each paragraph. Does the first sentence tell what the topic of the paragraph is? Do the rest of the sentences explain or support that main idea? Are there any sentences that should be moved to a different paragraph? Does each paragraph lead logically into the next one? Have you used transition words within the paragraph to improve the flow?

The individual sentences could also use some attention. Are they different lengths, and do they use a variety of sentence structures? Is the average sentence length 15 words or fewer? How many of them are in passive voice? Do you notice any jargon, idioms, nominalizations, or long phrases that can be shortened? Keep in mind that not all of your readers may have English as their first language.

Copy Editing

You can begin copy editing once all your ideas are in order. In this step, you will mainly look at spelling and grammar errors as well as the syntax and word choice. Even small errors can damage your credibility; people won't take your efforts seriously.

Definitely run your document through a spelling checker and a grammar checker, but remember not to rely on them for all your copy editing—they can't catch every single error. For instance, a spelling checker will not flag a word as misspelled if it is a real word. If you use "aloud" instead of "allowed," most spelling checkers will not notice it.

This is the stage where you can really use a professional editor for longer documents, if one is available to you. Many freelance editors work at this level of editing, although some of them will also do structural editing if you ask for it and pay for it. Make sure that your editor understands what you need and what you will expect them to do.

Proofreading

Proofreading is the final check for errors and typos. You can do this yourself before sending it to a proofreader to check it again, or you can rely on an editor or a proofreader to identify errors for you. If you are not able to hire a professional proofreader or editor, you can always ask a friend or a family member. My mother proofread this book for me! I hope she has done a good job.

First, make sure that there are no spelling or numerical errors in your document. This includes contact information such as emails, websites, and addresses. Having someone's name spelled correctly is a must. Think about how you feel when someone gets *your* name wrong. You can check the spelling of names on a company's website or a business site like LinkedIn.

Make sure that you're writing in the correct variant of English. English in the UK is different from American English. They spell some words in different ways and have different standards for punctuation. Your word processing program should have a function that allows you to choose which version of English you want. This is usually all you would need to do. Programs such as Grammarly can also help you with this.

Something that is really important when you proofread a document is checking to see that all the numbers are correct. This includes numbers for phone numbers, P.O. box numbers, order numbers, costs, etc. Be very careful with this, especially if you're supplying essential information. You don't want to increase the number of complaints your company receives because you supplied customers with incorrect information.

House Style and Style Guide

House style means the way your company does things when it comes to writing. It will include items such as the official name of the organization and whether they want it written out in full or if an abbreviation is okay. If the company has a preference for any grammar, spelling, or punctuation rules, the house style guide will include them. For example, some companies prefer to use Ms. instead of Mrs. or Miss.

Keep your business style guide or house style in mind when writing your document, but especially when you edit and proofread. If your organization doesn't have one, think about developing one, especially if you have many different people who produce documents in your business. This can help you ensure that all your communication has the same tone and voice and that the layout of documents is also universal. A style guide can benefit both large and small businesses.

If you're a sole entrepreneur, you can develop a style guide for yourself that will serve as a reminder when you write, edit, and proofread documents. Make notes on the mistakes you make frequently and develop a checklist for them. For example, if you know you have difficulty spelling certain words, make a list of them that you can refer to as you write. Keep it in a file on your computer or print it out so you'll always have it when you write.

Benefits of a Style Guide

It's essential to have some writing guidelines if you have many people working on different types of communication that will portray the image of your company. It's also useful for freelance writers, editors, proofreaders, and translators who don't work full time for your business. It will save a lot of time if they can work in your specific style from the beginning, and their documents don't have to be changed too much after they submit them.

Small matters such as font size, alternate spellings, or heading styles may not seem important, but if all your documents are in different styles, you're going to have an unprofessional, untidy image. Visual elements create your business's personality.

You should develop your business' identity around the audience you want to target. Are you marketing a product that will be sold to parents of small children? You will want to produce advertisements that appeal to that audience, with kid-friendly graphics and typefaces. If you're providing a service to other businesses, you'll want a more formal yet straightforward style.

This can be a problem if you have different people updating your company website, for example. Remember that when you look for consistency, you should consider digital content as well.

If your employees use a style guide while writing, it will save a lot of time—they won't have to be constantly asking each other questions about what grammar or punctuation to use. You could even have word lists. Decide on which business-specific words and terms you want to use in your communication and which you want to avoid.

Creating Your Style Guide

When you start developing your style guide, it's up to you and your coworkers to decide what you want to include. It's a good idea to speak to people who have been with the business or company for a while, and have a good idea of what image the company wants to convey.

Your style guide can be either long or short, but people are more likely to consult a short guide. People who aren't experienced writers might be put off by a thick book that resembles a dictionary.

If your business employs editors or writers or has an ongoing relationship with a freelance editor, get input from them as well. They will be up to date with the latest information on plain language and other grammar rules. You can even hire an editor to create a house style guide for you.

It's also important to adjust your style guide as your business changes and grows. Corporate identity is how you present yourself to your audience, and it includes visual elements such as your logos, the colors you use in your communication, product packaging, and your advertising and marketing techniques. Remember that if you change the corporate identity of your business, your style guide will have to be updated as well.

Before creating your own style guide, look at existing guides and dictionaries. If you work in a very specific industry, look at style guides for this industry. For example, the *Chicago Manual of Style* and the *AP Stylebook* are well-known style guides that can help you a great deal when it comes to business writing or technical writing.

Obviously, you can't cover everything in your guide, so focus on what is appropriate for your company. Consider the type of language and situations that are related to your business. Include acronyms and jargon that are specific to your industry. For example, if you are part of the printing industry, you will want to cover common terms like "Pantone," "CMYK," and "crop marks."

Checklist for a Plain English Style Guide

Check the box to make sure you have included the items below in your plain English style guide.

Have you included average word counts for sentences and paragraphs?	
Have you included terminology and jargon lists for your profession or industry? Are there words your editors or writers shouldn't use? Did you include explanations in your style guide that will help lay people understand the jargon you use?	
Which dialect of English should you use? Do you need American, UK, or Australian English? Have you set your word processing program to use the correct form of English?	
Did you remember to include how your organization's name should be spelled and whether text like "LLC" should be used after the name?	
Have you made sure that the writing of the guide conforms to plain English conventions? For example, did you use familiar words and cut long sentences? Have you used easy grammatical structures?	

Key Takeaways

- It's important to review your writing before you publish, print, or send it.
- If you are editing by yourself, there are many ways to review your writing: leaving it alone for a while, reading it out loud, trying it out with a focus group, using software tools, or hiring a professional editor or proofreader.
- There are three steps in the editing process: structural editing, copy editing, and proofreading. During each of these stages, you look for different kinds of errors.
- In structural editing, you want to make sure that your ideas flow naturally and are supported.
- In copy editing, you look for mistakes in grammar, spelling, syntax, and word choice.
- Proofreading is the final stage of reviewing your writing. When you proofread, you make sure that there are no mistakes or typos.
- Having a style guide or house style will help make sure that everyone in your organization uses the same standards. You can develop your own house style guide or use a good one like the *Chicago Manual of Style* of *AP Stylebook*.
- A checklist of the main principles of plain English can help you review your writing for readability and clarity.

In Chapter 8, we'll look at how checklists and templates can make business writing easier.

CHAPTER 8

Plain English Checklist and Templates

Once you've done your research about plain English writing and you're ready to start writing, it's useful to have templates and a checklist to help you on your way.

Even if you're pretty sure you managed to get your ideas down in simple and clear English, it's useful to have examples and a checklist to help you make sure you get it right.

What's a Template?

The purpose of a template is to streamline communications. A template is like a form you fill in to produce a document. It is set up so that all your styles for text and headings—the fonts, line spacing, etc.—are in place where they need to be. It acts as a reminder of how you want your document to look. And it provides a place for you to fill in your information without worrying about those aspects of the document.

A template should also contain elements that don't change from document to document, such as your company's logo or your signature and contact information. Each of your employees that write emails, for example, can have a separate template with their own official information.

Checklist

You know how valuable checklists are in business. A checklist can help a manager make sure that employees are following procedures. It can help employees make sure that their work meets standards. A checklist for your writing and your documents is no different. It will help you be sure that your writing is in line with the principles of plain English, which will make your documents easier to read and understand. In other words, a checklist is a quick way to check the quality of your writing.

Once you've written your document, before you hand it to an editor or your readers, check that it meets the following standards.

It has been written with your audience in mind. The word level isn't too high and is understandable for the average reader. You speak directly to your readers by using the pronoun "you."	
The layout of your document makes it easier for readers to understand. For example, headings should make it easy to follow the structure of the text. Bullet lists can make your document easier to read.	
Coworkers have provided input, especially people who are knowledgeable about the area your document addresses. You have used a focus group to uncover potential problems.	
The document uses mostly simple tenses and basic grammatical structures. Compound-complex sentences are used sparingly.	
Make sure that you've shortened sentences by leaving out unnecessary words. The words you've used are familiar to your readers.	

You've included graphics, infographics, tables, and lists to explain complicated content, if necessary.	

Business Emails

Email is one of the main ways of business communication today, especially since so many people started working from home during the COVID-19 pandemic, and this trend promises to continue into the future. Email has made it quicker and easier to communicate with coworkers, employees, and customers around the globe. However, there are some rules when it comes to writing clear emails that get your message across effectively.

While emails can be less formal than other business communications, you still have to follow normal grammar rules. The message might be confusing if you use slang or an inappropriate tone. It's best to follow a familiar format, as this will encourage your reader to keep on reading. They will know that important information is coming, but that it will be presented to them in a familiar and understandable format.

Tips for Writing Emails

There are many ways to make your emails easier for your audience to understand and to communicate more effectively with them. In addition to using plain English, these tips can improve the response you receive from your emails.

- Never use the shortcuts like people do in text messaging. This is not appropriate for a business context, and many people won't understand what you mean. For example, don't use "2" instead of "to" or "btw" instead of "by the way." Even if you do send text messages, keep them professional.

- Make sure that you put people's names in the right fields, so that readers will know who is receiving the messages. For example, the name of the primary person or people who need to see the email should be placed in the "To" field. Use the "CC" or carbon copy field to share the information with recipients who may need a copy for their files but aren't expected to respond directly.
- Use "BCC" or blind carbon copy when you want to copy someone on an email without other recipients knowing.
- Your emails should be as short as possible. If you need to send a lengthy report, for example, attach the document to your email describing what the report contains.
- Keep your email Subject field short. This makes them easier for people to remember and to find again when they need them later.
- Don't make your formal emails appear less serious by using emojis or emoticons .
- If you are replying to an email, make sure that you respond to everything raised in it. That way, you'll avoid back-and-forth emails and even complaints.
- Another way to make life easier for your customers is not to attach huge audio or video files that might crash their email system.
- Make sure you virus scan everything you send out. Your email program may do this automatically, but you should check to see that it does.
- Avoid using the high priority option when you don't need to. You may think you'll get a better response, but no one will pay attention to your truly urgent emails if you overuse this function.

The Formal Email

Here's an example of a formal email:

Dear Juan,

I hope you are doing well.

Could we please set up a meeting to discuss the issue in more detail? Let me know what day and time will suit you, so we can discuss the matter in person.

Paula wishes to attend the meeting as well, so I will find a date and time that is suitable for everyone.

Please let me know if you have any questions.

Kind regards,

Benjamin

Formal Email Template

You can use a template like this one for a formal email. You may want to include a bold-faced heading for the first or middle section to emphasize the topic noted in the subject line. Your reader's eyes will be drawn to this information.

To [recipient]:

Subject:

Dear [recipient's name],

First Section [heading, if desired]

The first section should be short and state all the facts. Are you inquiring about something or are you sharing information? Include all the most important information in this paragraph.

Middle Section [heading, if desired]

This paragraph (or paragraphs) can give more information related to the first paragraph.

Final paragraph

Here you can thank your email recipient for their time and include a call to action, if necessary. This can help you achieve what you set out to do in writing the email.

Closing

End your email with "Best wishes," "Kind regards," "Sincerely," or another polite phrase.

[Signature]

Your name and contact information.

Informal Email

Some business communications can be handled with a more informal email. These might include emails that go to coworkers at the same organizational level as you and ones that go to people you know well or outside of the office. Using the principles of plain English is still a good idea. Long, complicated sentences can be difficult for anyone to read. You can use more jargon related to your field if you are sure that the person understands it.

Here's an example:

Marie:

Thanks for letting me know about the birthday party on Wednesday. I should be able to make it unless the deadline for the Jefferson project moves up.

Will the whole IT department be attending or just the team leaders? Should we bring gifts, or are we just going to pick up the check for Brad's lunch?

Let me know.

Jaleel

Informal Email Template

To [recipient]:

Subject:

Greeting:

The greeting can be informal and is followed by a colon rather than a comma.

[Body Text]

The body text can also be informal. You should use separate paragraphs for different parts of the email. The final paragraph can be a call to action if you expect a response.

[Signature]

You can use your first name or first name and initial if there is more than one person with the same first name in the organization.

Business Letter

Occasionally, you will need to write a business letter if an email just won't suit the occasion. Business letters need to be in plain English. You will get your message across faster, and people are more inclined to keep on reading when they can follow your logic and don't have to figure out complicated language. If you follow this process to create your plain English business letters, you shouldn't have a problem when it comes to getting your message across.

First, you need to decide what the goal of your letter is. This will help you to write more clearly and get your message across in a straightforward way. For example, a letter to a valued customer will be written very differently from a warning letter you send to an employee or a letter of dismissal.

Before you start writing your letter, make sure that you have all the information to help you get this done as quickly and successfully as possible. For example, you need copies of a customer's complaints if you're writing to apologize to them. If you're going to discipline one of your employees, you need to have a good understanding of what they did wrong. Never write business letters based on assumptions.

Your letter should include the following details:

- your name and address
- date
- name and address of the recipient
- greeting
- body
- closing
- signature

Example of a Business Letter

One of the most common business letters that you may need to write is the letter of application for a job. You don't have to include too much information in this kind of letter because it is a "cover letter" which will be sent along with your resume.

When it comes to application letters, Human Resources Departments can get hundreds or even thousands of applications for the same job. The applications that are easy to understand and have a clear layout are most likely to make it to the top of the pile to be reviewed. Never write a long letter that gives the same information as your resume.

Personalize the greeting if you can. Go online to the company's website to learn the name of the HR Director who has posted the position. It will make a much better impression than a letter addressed to the generic "Human Resources Director."

January 25, 2023

Karen Taylor

678 Fairfield Blvd.

Chicago, IL 60611

Ms. Annabel Stapleton

123 South 45th St.

Chicago, IL 60611

Dear Ms. Stapleton,

I am applying for the position of Editorial Content Writer. My resume is attached.

My 10 years of experience as a freelance writer, working for clients in business, as well as writing reviews, blogs, educational, and instructional articles, demonstrate my reliability and flexibility. Combined with my positive work ethic, this should make me a prime candidate for this position.

I can work on-site or from home, whichever you prefer. I would be available to start immediately.

I look forward to hearing from you.

Sincerely,

Karen Taylor

k.taylor@email.com

Business Letter Template

[Date]

[Your name and address]

[Recipient's name and address]

[Greeting]

[First paragraph]

[Second paragraph]

[Additional paragraphs if needed.]

[Closing]

[Signature]

[Contact email]

Business Memo

Whether you own a business or you work for one, it's important to know how to write business memos that are easy to understand.

A good memo is short, to the point and can include a call to action. If a memo contains too much information in language that is difficult to understand, it won't be as effective.

Before you start writing, decide on the exact purpose of your memo. Most memos are to share information, but you might also use them for persuasion.

The purpose of the memo should be clear and descriptive in the subject line so that people know what it's about.

Business Memo

The heading segment follows this general format:

- TO: (recipient's names)
- CC: (whoever your copying on the memo)
- FROM: (sender's name and job title)
- DATE: (full current date)
- SUBJECT: (Re: specific topic)

Opening

Use at least a paragraph to create the background for what you want to discuss. Immediately state what you want to discuss.

Discussion

The discussion should be a more detailed description. Start with general information and then move on to more specific facts. You can use bulleted lists or other graphic layouts such as tables or pie charts if they will make the material more understandable.

Summary

If the memo is longer than one page, include the rest of the information as a separate attachment.

Closing

You can close your memo with a call to action. Clearly indicate the action you want your readers to take.

Business Memo Example

To: All Employees

From: Dale Rogers, Communications Manager

Date: April 2, 2023

Re: Using Plain English in Business Communication

In order to improve our communication inside and outside the company, we have decided that all staff need to adhere to plain English writing principles. Some of these principles include as follows:

- Use short sentences and simple words that are easy to understand.
- The purpose of your communication should be clear in your subject line.
- Make sure that the layouts of your communications are user-friendly, for example, by using bulleted lists, if applicable.
- Edit and proofread all communication before you send it out.

Ask the manager of your section if there are other rules that will apply to your department's communications. Training will be offered. The expectation is that everyone should be using plain English by next month.

Please contact me if you have specific questions.

Business Report

Business reports can be written for a number of different reasons. The aim of the report might be to inform your readers why you did certain things, what you discovered about a problem, or why a new policy was instituted.

Make sure most of these sections are included in your report: Title, Introduction, Discussion, and Conclusion. Some business reports are actually very long and include graphics and data. However, in general, reports are usually shorter and are sometimes written on a company template. Try to keep the message to one page, if you can. You can add a second page with more detail, if necessary. In the following example, for instance, you might want to have a separate page with a chart comparing the two years' results.

Example of Business Report
Accident Rates Decreasing

As you know, the company's Safety Committee has been examining our record regarding safety violations. We are pleased to report that there have been fewer accidents this year than last year and that none of the accidents resulted in serious harm.

Types of accidents this year

Most of the accidents that were reported were minor, including 20 slip-and-fall accidents resulting in scrapes and strains. Another 5 injuries were caused by failure of equipment, and 2 more were the result of failure to follow required safety procedures. Fortunately, these accidents were not severe, but the employees were required to take a safety class.

Comparisons to last year

At this time last year, there had been 31 slip-and-fall accidents, 7 equipment failures, and 3 incidents resulting from failing to follow safety procedures, for a total of 41 accidents. This year there have been only 27.

Conclusion

We are proud of the efforts that employees have been making to ensure a safe workplace. The Safety Committee deserves special mention for their outstanding work.

Let's make sure that this positive trend continues through the rest of the year.

Template for Business Report

[Title]

The title should make the recipient want to read the report.

[Introduction]

A brief explanation of the report's topic.

[Discussion]

Facts and figures or other supporting material.

[Conclusion]

Any final remarks, such as a summary, call to action, or acknowledgements.

[Additions]

A second page can be added for charts, graphs, or other less important information or explanations.

Conclusion

Now that you've learned about plain English, you can see how it can improve your business life, academic life—even your personal life. You can use the basic principles in any of your written communications, from business memos to your family holiday letters. The people who receive them will be able to understand them more easily, and you'll feel good about your new-found ability to communicate more effectively. It's a win-win situation!

Plain English is easier to write as well as easier to read. You don't have to worry about mastering complicated grammar; long, involved sentences; and difficult sentence and paragraph structure. You'll be more comfortable and confident once you try using plain English in your everyday writing.

You'll know that any audience can understand your communications. There are a lot of people in the world whose first language is not English or who have not finished their education. They're very important to reach, and plain English is the best way to connect with them.

Plain English is especially important in the workplace. Clear communication is vital for growing your business, reaching your customers, and coordinating your workforce. Even if you're not the owner or president of a business, plain English will help your work life run more smoothly. There will be fewer misunderstandings and better coordination with your coworkers.

One of the most important things you can do to improve your communications skills is to plan your writing. Knowing what you need and want to say is the first step in making plain English work for you. Setting out your ideas in a logical manner before you start writing will help a lot, whether you create a formal outline or not. After that, you need to understand how to format and lay out your document for maximum readability.

Another vital aspect of plain English writing is thinking about your intended readers. What do they need to know? What will be their expectations? What is their level of expertise with the English language? How likely are they to understand the technical terms associated with the subject you're writing about? Have you addressed them directly and in a positive tone?

Grammar, sentence structure, capitalization, and punctuation are not just a lot of dry, difficult rules that you have to memorize. They're a way to make your writing correct, but they're also a way to make your writing easily understandable. Properly written sentences simply convey more precise meaning than sentences with improper mechanics. For example, run-on sentences that don't connect clauses properly can be confusing. If you understand grammar and sentence structure, you will be better able to write texts that vary in length and are more interesting to read.

In plain English writing, you don't risk confusing your readers with obscure jargon, idioms, and clichés. Instead, you use clear, understandable words and avoid adding extra articles and prepositions to your sentences. Keeping your readers' level of experience in mind will be a big help in creating text that they can relate to.

Before you publish, print, or send your writing, it's important to review it to make sure it doesn't contain mistakes. You can read your writing aloud, which will help you spot typos and sentences that are too long or unclear. You could also recruit test readers from your intended audience. If they have an easy time reading and understanding your text, you can be more confident that it will be effective.

Another strategy that will help in creating professional-looking and effective communications is to use templates in preparing them. Templates for a document allow you to fill in information like you would when filling in a form. Your structure and formatting will be done in advance and you can use the same template again and again to make all your communications consistent.

With all these tools at your command, you will be able to produce effective communications in plain English that anyone can read and understand. No matter whether you work in a large business, a small office, or for yourself at home, you'll write so that any audience will get your meaning quickly. You'll sound more professional and have more confidence in your ability to write well. The benefits you will experience include better customer response and satisfaction, greater clarity in your emails and reports, and enhanced understanding of everything you write.

If this book has helped you improve your writing and your ability to produce documents that are both correct and effective, we encourage you to leave an online review telling us about your success. We'd love to hear from you!

If you are interested, please stay connected with my books and resources by heading to my website - www.grammatika.net.au

Glossary

- **Acronym:** A form of abbreviation using the first letters of each word in a phrase.
- **Active voice:** A sentence structure in which the subject of the sentence performs an action indicated by an action verb.
- **BCC:** Blind carbon copy; a copy of an email sent to an address that is not visible to other recipients.
- **CC:** Carbon copy; a copy of an email sent to more than one recipient.
- **Cliche:** A word or phrase that is used so often that it becomes trite.
- **Complex sentence:** A sentence that contains at least one independent clause and one dependent clause.
- **Compound sentence:** A sentence that contains two independent clauses joined by a comma and a conjunction.
- **Compound-complex sentence:** A sentence that contains an independent clause and two dependent clauses.
- **Copy edit:** To edit a document looking at sentence structure, spelling, and grammar.
- **Dependent clause:** A clause that does not contain both a subject and a verb.
- **Double negative:** Using two or more negative words such as can't, won't, never, no, not in a single sentence.
- **Font:** A typeface that includes all the letters of an alphabet, numbers, and special characters; can be serif or sans serif.

- **Gerund:** A noun formed by adding -ing to a verb.
- **Idioms:** Phrases that use words in a nonliteral fashion to convey a colloquial meaning.
- **Independent clause:** A clause that contains both a subject and a verb.
- **Infographic:** A way of sharing information that includes both visual elements and text.
- **Jargon:** Language that is specific to a certain field or profession, but is not generally understood by laypeople.
- **Layout:** How a document is formatted, including textual and visual elements.
- **Nominalization:** Creating a noun from another part of speech such as a verb or adjective.
- **Passive voice:** Sentence structure with the subject of the verb being acted upon.
- **Plain English:** Writing that features simple, easy-to-follow sentences and is easy to understand; language that does not contain difficult words or phrases or complicated structures.
- **Run-on sentence:** A sentence containing two or more independent clauses separated only by a comma.
- **Sans Serif:** Describes a typeface that does not contain small projections on the strokes of each letter.
- **Serif:** Describes a typeface that contains small projections on the strokes of each letter.
- **Simple sentence:** A sentence that contains one subject and one verb; an independent clause.
- **SVO:** Subject-verb-object word order; the basic pattern for simple English sentences.

- **Template:** An example of a document including elements such as typeface, line spacing, headings, etc., to be filled in by the user.
- **Title case:** The use of capital letters to begin each word in a phrase or sentence with the exception of articles and prepositions of under four letters.
- **Typeface:** A font that includes all the letters of an alphabet, numbers, and special characters; can be serif or sans serif.

About the Author

Nicole Foster is a registered high school English and Literacy teacher with an additional major in Adult Education. Nicole taught at schools in Australia, before working overseas at schools in Singapore and Brunei. Nicole then went on to teach English for Aerospace Engineering at two universities in Thailand, before returning to Australia. With a M.Ed. in TESOL, Nicole has a personal interest in contributing to active research in Pasifika Education. She teaches literacy and numeracy across the curriculum in Australia, assisting teachers, students and businesses to simplify their writing.

Outside of work life, the author is a busy mother of a teenage son and a two-year-old puppy. On the weekends, she can be found at the beach.

References

A to Z of legal phrases. (n.d.). Plainenglish.co.uk. Retrieved November 24, 2022, from http://plainenglish.co.uk/a-to-z-of-legal-phrases.html

Bailey, P., Tuinman, J. J., & Jones, S. (2013, December 16). *Literacy.* The Canadian Encyclopedia. https://www.thecanadianencyclopedia.ca/en/article/literacy#:~:text=Measure%20of%20Literacy

Buck, L. (2016, August 17). *The need for plain English in global business.* Resources for English Language Learners and Teachers. Pearson English. https://www.english.com/blog/plain-english-in-business/

CBC Radio. (2021, July 9). *Nearly half of adult Canadians struggle with literacy — and that's bad for the economy.* CBC. https://www.cbc.ca/radio/costofliving/let-s-get-digital-from-bitcoin-to-stocktok-plus-what-low-literacy-means-for-canada-s-economy-1.5873703/nearly-half-of-adult-canadians-struggle-with-literacy-and-that-s-bad-for-the-economy-1.5873757

Chris, A. (2022, April 29). *10 best online digital marketing degrees (Bachelors & masters).* Reliablesoft.net. https://www.reliablesoft.net/best-digital-marketing-degrees/

Creating a house style for your content: Why & how? (2016, May 5). TheEword Blog. https://www.theeword.co.uk/blog/creating-a-house-style-for-your-content-why-how/

Dingwall, J. R., Labrie, C., McLennon, T., & Underwood, L. (n.d.). *Grammar and punctuation.*

Ecampusontario.pressbooks.pub. https://ecampusontario.pressbooks.pub/profcommsontario/chapter/grammar-and-punctuation/

Doran, M. (2021, November 30). Council post: Why and how to use plain language in your corporate disclosure. *Forbes.* https://www.forbes.com/sites/forbescommunicationscouncil/2021/11/30/why-and-how-to-use-plain-language-in-your-corporate-disclosure/?sh=477e1217d913

Erwin, K. (2021, December 8). *Professional email templates: Email formatting & examples.* Mailshake. https://mailshake.com/blog/professional-email-templates/

5 reasons to use plain language. (2012, October 22). Writers Write. https://www.writerswrite.co.za/five-reasons-to-use-plain-language/

5 reasons why grammar is important in writing. (n.d.). Prowritingaid.com. https://prowritingaid.com/why-is-grammar-important-in-writing

48+ US literacy statistics 2022 - Percentage by state. (2022, November 18). THINKIMPACT. https://www.thinkimpact.com/literacy-statistics/

Garnier, L. (2021, November 12). *Zombie nouns: What are nominalizations?* BKA Content. https://www.bkacontent.com/gs-zombie-nouns-what-are-nominalizations/

Gov/Easytoread -2 -. (n.d.). *Easy-to-read NYC guidelines for clear and effective communication.* Mayor's Office of Adult Education Mayor's Office of Immigrant Affairs Easy-to-Read NYC Guidelines for Clear and Effective

Communication. Retrieved December 1, 2022, from https://www.nyc.gov/html/adulted/downloads/pdf/easy-to-read-nyc.pdf

Greater Good in Education. (n.d.). *SEL for adults: Self-awareness and self-management*. Greater Good in Education. https://ggie.berkeley.edu/my-well-being/sel-for-adults-self-awareness-and-self-management/

Griffis, G. (2022, January 31). *How to make a style guide: The process and examples you need*. GatherContent. https://gathercontent.com/blog/how-to-make-a-style-guide-that-people-will-actually-use

Holden, D. (2019, September 20). *Benefits of plain English writing and editing for business and government*. Central Editing. https://www.centralediting.com.au/plain-english-writing/

How to write in plain English (with examples). (2022, September 13). Proofed. https://proofed.co.uk/writing-tips/how-to-write-in-plain-english-with-examples/

Indeed Editorial Team. (2022, June 16). *45 business jargon terms and phrases (with example sentences)*. Indeed Career Guide. https://www.indeed.com/career-advice/career-development/jargons-in-business

Interpreters and Translators, Inc. (2021, June 15). *The importance of plain language in business*. MarTech Health. https://martech.health/articles/the-importance-of-plain-language-in-business

James, A. (2011, August 24). *How to write a "plain English" business plan*. Kariti. https://klariti.com/2011/08/24/simple-business-plan/

Kramer, L. (2016, August 15). *Top 10 principles for plain language.* National Archives. https://www.archives.gov/open/plain-writing/10-principles.html

Language Tool. (2021, December 3). *Why you shouldn't use double negatives.* LanguageTool Insights. https://languagetool.org/insights/post/double-negatives/

Lyons, D. (2021, March 10). How many people speak English, and where is it spoken? *Babbel Magazine.* https://www.babbel.com/en/magazine/how-many-people-speak-english-and-where-is-it-spoken

Majewski, J. (2021, May 10). *Why is grammar important in writing: Plus our top 3 reasons.* When You Write. https://whenyouwrite.com/why-is-grammar-important/

Medical information. (n.d.). Plainenglish.co.uk. Retrieved November 24, 2022, from http://plainenglish.co.uk/medical-information.html

Newman, J. (2009, November 12). *Technical writing: Business letter.* Lupinworks. https://www.lupinworks.com/roche/pages/busLetter.php

Nordquist, R. (2019, May 24). *What does nominalization mean in English grammar?* ThoughtCo. https://www.thoughtco.com/nominalization-in-grammar-1691430

Peachy Essay. (2021, May 11). *Importance of grammar in writing – Complete guide.* Peachyessay. https://peachyessay.com/blogs/importance-of-grammar-in-writing/

Plain language. (n.d.). Writer. https://writer.com/guides/plain-language/

Provost, R. (2022, January 30). *Elements of sentence structure explained.* StudioBinder. https://www.studiobinder.com/blog/what-is-sentence-structure-examples/

Punctuation and capitalisation | Style Manual. (2021, November 6). Www.stylemanual.gov.au. https://www.stylemanual.gov.au/grammar-punctuation-and-conventions/punctuation-and-capitalisation

Punctuation and capitalization: A simple guide with examples. (2019, June 3). Teachingutopians. https://teachingutopians.com/2019/06/03/punctuation-and-capitalization-a-simple-guide-with-examples/

Rahman, A. (2019, December 5). The pointlessness of using difficult words. *The Daily Star.* https://www.thedailystar.net/shout/news/the-pointlessness-using-difficult-words-1835968

Ripper, L. (2014, November 17). *FAQs.* Laura Ripper Copy-Editing and Proofreading. https://lauraripperproofreading.com/services/plain-english-editing/faqs/

Romani, B. (2020, May 30). *Word order rules in English - A comprehensive guide.* Scientific Editing. https://www.scientific-editing.info/blog/word-order-rules-in-english/

Sentence structure | Communication for professionals. (n.d.). Lumen. https://courses.lumenlearning.com/suny-esc-communicationforprofessionals/chapter/sentence-structure/

Sparano, R. (2021, March 2). *Why plain language is right for business.* Plainlli. https://plainlii.com/2021/03/02/why-plain-language-is-right-for-business/

Translators Without Borders. (2020, October 13). *Plain language tips for writers and translators.* Translators Without Borders Blog. https://translatorswithoutborders.org/blog/eight-plain-language-tips-for-writers-and-translators-on-international-plain-language-day/

University of Kent. (n.d.). *How to write in plain English.* University of Kent. https://www.kent.ac.uk/guides/plain-english

Vágvölgyi, R., Coldea, A., Dresler, T., Schrader, J., & Nuerk, H.-C. (2016). A review about functional illiteracy: Definition, cognitive, linguistic, and numerical aspects. *Frontiers in Psychology, 7.* https://doi.org/10.3389/fpsyg.2016.01617

Vozza, S. (2022, March 16). *Using big words can make you look smart, but only if you do this.* Fast Company. https://www.fastcompany.com/90729952/using-big-words-can-make-you-look-smart-but-only-if-you-do-this

Walden University. (2009). *Academic guides: Scholarly voice: Varying sentence structure.* Waldenu.edu. https://academicguides.waldenu.edu/writingcenter/scholarlyvoice/sentencestructure

Wright, E. (2013, June 5). *What are the benefits of a house style guide?* Erin Wright Writing. https://erinwrightwriting.com/in-house-style-guides-for-small-businesses-benefits-preparation/

Yang, B. (2019, June 26). *Web writing style guide.* Library.duke.edu. https://library.duke.edu/about/writing-styleguide

Made in the USA
Monee, IL
28 April 2026

49136482R00080